Endorsements for this book

"A compelling read!

"With truth, reparations, racial healing, and reimagining public safety initiatives in hundreds of municipalities, *Cousins* is a story that could not be more timely."

—FANIA E. DAVIS, SOCIAL JUSTICE ACTIVIST,
CIVIL RIGHTS ATTORNEY, RESTORATIVE JUSTICE LEADER

◈

"I LOVE *Cousins*. A must-read for everyone committed to racial healing and justice.

"Betty's and Phoebe's lives couldn't have been more different, growing up. The legacy of slavery looms large here. Yet once they found each other, they committed to healing and repair and to building an authentic and accountable friendship.

"A powerful book!"

—THOMAS NORMAN DEWOLF, AUTHOR OF *INHERITING THE TRADE*, CO-AUTHOR OF *GATHER AT THE TABLE* AND *THE LITTLE BOOK OF RACIAL HEALING*; CO-MANAGER OF COMING TO THE TABLE

Endorsements for this book

"A completely unpredictable roller coaster of a book that will break your heart, warm your heart, make you enraged, teach you about dialogue, and ultimately deepen your belief in the potential of racial reconciliation.

"Beyond the expert craftsmanship of the text, the honesty and vulnerability of the authors beautifully reflect the courage and compassion that will be needed by many more people if we are ever to embark on a sustainable journey of racial reckoning."

—DR. DAVID WILEY CAMPT, PRINCIPAL OF THE DIALOGUE
COMPANY AND CREATOR OF THE WHITE ALLY TOOLKIT

❖

"How can America begin to address its legacy of slavery and racism? This very engaging book tells the courageous journey of these two cousins—one Black, one White—to discover and overcome their connected pasts. It suggests a way to forge a healing pathway toward a hopeful future.

"Their story offers inspiration for others to undertake their own journeys, as well as concrete resources for doing so. Highly recommended."

—HOWARD ZEHR, PIONEER IN RESTORATIVE JUSTICE, AUTHOR OF
CHANGING LENSES AND THE LITTLE BOOK OF RESTORATIVE JUSTICE,
DISTINGUISHED PROFESSOR OF RESTORATIVE JUSTICE AT EASTERN
MENNONITE UNIVERSITY'S CENTER FOR JUSTICE AND PEACEBUILDING

❖

"*Cousins* is a riveting story, highlighting the possibility of healing. The openness and vulnerability with which Betty and Phoebe share their stories will capture you.

"The journey they invite us on is a story that everyone needs to read."

—JODIE GEDDES, CO-MANAGER OF COMING TO THE
TABLE, A COMMUNITY ORGANIZER, AND CO-AUTHOR
OF THE LITTLE BOOK OF RACIAL HEALING

"I hope the experiences of Betty and Phoebe will inspire others to sit down at the table of sisterhood and brotherhood to promote racial healing."

—U.S. Senator Tim Kaine of Virginia

Endorsements for this book

"*Cousins* is a wonderful book! I was charmed by the story of these two amazing women. How marvelous that, in this time of endless separation, two people came together across so many barriers to build new bridges for healing old wounds.

"Its crisp and familial tone resonated with me—actually, it embraced me—like a long-lost friend. *Cousins* is a salve—a smooth, comfortable healing for the rough spots we face when reconciling a difficult past.

"*Cousins* is stunningly rich with hometown history, waiting to be healed. It both weeps with racial conflict and wails with brave conviction. Phoebe and Betty carry their blended story beautifully, taking us through the gray areas and safely bringing us home.

"A marvelous blueprint for anyone seeking to mend the past and redefine family."

—DANITA ROUNTREE GREEN, TRAUMA
HEALING FACILITATOR AND PLAYWRIGHT

COUSINS

"This powerful book weaves together the eloquent stories of two impressive women—stories of survival, determination, and awakening, of honesty, spirituality, and success.

"They give us a detective story and a mystery, a reconciliation and a celebration. A reader will be grateful for all of them."

—EDWARD L. AYERS, RECIPIENT OF
THE NATIONAL HUMANITIES MEDAL
FROM PRESIDENT BARACK OBAMA

COUSINS

Connected through slavery,
a Black woman and a White woman
discover their past—and each other

Betty Kilby Baldwin & Phoebe Kilby

WALNUT
STREET
BOOKS
LANCASTER,
PENNSYLVANIA

walnutstreetbooks.com

We dedicate this book to Sarah and Juliet, and to Juliet's children Simon, James, John, and Sarah, born enslaved but surviving to create the roots of a thriving tree of descendants. And to all their descendants, including those now benefiting from the Kilby Family Endowed Scholarship Fund.

SPECIAL NOTE —

THE AUTHORS' PROCEEDS from this book will be donated to the Kilby Family Endowed Scholarship Fund, a reparations project which Phoebe and Betty conceived of together.

The Kilby Family Endowed Scholarship Fund provides scholarships to descendants of persons enslaved in Culpeper, Rappahannock, and Madison counties, Virginia, prior to the end of the Civil War in 1865.

Preference is given to descendants of persons enslaved by John Kilby of Culpeper County, VA (1715-1772), and by his lineal descendants who were enslavers.

"This endowment was established to honor these enslaved persons and their descendants in recognition of their strength and resilience, and to contribute to making amends for their mistreatment."

Readers are invited to contribute to this endowment: poisefoundation.org/kilby family endowed scholarship fund

Thank you.

CONTENTS

1. Two Women... Two Vastly Different Lives   3
    BETTY AND PHOEBE

2. A Child's Point of View   9
    BETTY

3. War is Not the Answer   17
    PHOEBE

4. Soldiers Without Uniforms   29
    BETTY

5. Family Secrets   55
    PHOEBE

6. Hello, Cousin!   69
    BETTY AND PHOEBE

7. Dinner and a Movie   78
    BETTY AND PHOEBE

8. Love, War, and Peace   89
    BETTY

9. Aunt Lucia and Cousin Tim   101
    PHOEBE

10. The Forever Fight   115
    BETTY AND PHOEBE

11. Sojourner Truth in Kalamazoo   134
    BETTY

12. Communing with the Ancestors 142
PHOEBE

13. Coming to the Table 152
BETTY AND PHOEBE

14. I Am Free! 169
BETTY

15. Complicity in the Oppression 177
PHOEBE

16. Together on the Road 192
BETTY AND PHOEBE

17. Q&A with Betty and Phoebe 205

18. Repairing the Harms 221
BETTY AND PHOEBE

Readings and Sources 238

Acknowledgments 242

Also From Walnut Street Books 243

About the Authors 244

TWO WOMEN... TWO VASTLY DIFFERENT LIVES

BETTY AND PHOEBE

1

Two women, Betty and Phoebe—one African American, one Euro-pean American—met for the first time in 2007. Though they both were born with the same last name, they knew nothing of each other prior to that time. They had lived vastly different lives.

BETTY KILBY FISHER BALDWIN: I am the third of five children. I was the first and only girl for all of three years and one month. When my sister Pat arrived, I lost that special place in the family. In fact, after that, I could not find anything special about me.

Daddy was like me. He didn't have a special place in his family either. We were both the third child in our families. Neither one of us could sing; neither of us could carry a tune. We both had a longing to find our place. There was something about me that made me want to be like him. I longed to be like him.

With a third-grade education, Daddy couldn't read very well, but he always read the newspaper out loud. Sometimes when he didn't know the words, he would have my brothers Jimmy or John tell him the words. By the time it was my time to help him with the words, he was reading pretty good.

Daddy bought 52 acres of land in Happy Creek, just outside of Front Royal, Virginia. I was about six years old when he built a house on that land. I had to share a

Betty Kilby at 12.

room with my little sister. The boys, Jimmy and John, shared a room. When my brother Gene was old enough, Momma moved him upstairs to sleep in the room with the big boys.

Daddy built a barn and bought milk cows. He taught Jimmy and John how to milk the cows by hand. As they increased their milking skills, the number of milk cows increased. Daddy was always thinking and planning. We graduated to 50 head of cattle and two milking machines. That was really exciting since we were the only ones in the neighborhood with milking machines.

My job was feeding the chickens and collecting the eggs. Naturally, as we got older, our jobs on the farm changed and increased. Not only did our jobs change and increase, so did Daddy's. He worked a full-time job at the American Viscose manufacturing plant as a janitor *and* managed our farm work. We were expected to do no less.

We had to work as hard as Daddy and Momma. We had school, the garden, and our farm chores. When we complained about all work and no play, Daddy would say, "You better stay in school and get an education, or *this* will be your life's work."

I guess Daddy was listening to himself talk, since our educational opportunities didn't look so good.

JANET O. "PHOEBE" KILBY: I was born in 1952 in Baltimore, Maryland. I lived in the city, not the suburbs, just down the street from the mayor, Mayor Thomas D'Alessandro III, the brother of Nancy Pelosi. It was a neighborhood of doctors, lawyers, and financiers. My sister, friends, and I roller-skated in the street and played in the beautiful public gardens. We also liked to ride our bicycles to the Baltimore Museum of Art, where

Phoebe Kilby at about 5.

we spent our time looking at the paintings of all the horses that had won the Preakness.

Most people today think of Baltimore as the majority-Black city it is with many racial problems, like the death of Freddie Gray when he was in police custody, and the riots afterwards. But most of the time I lived there, Baltimore was still majority-White.

BETTY: All we had was a school that had classes through the seventh grade, and my brother Jimmy was nearing the end of his schooling as far as we could see. One day as I was sitting in the kitchen peeling peaches to can, I asked point blank, "Well, Daddy, where we gonna send Jimmy to get an education?"

He looked at me real strange and said, "Are you Jimmy's momma? That's my business and you are still a child."

I left that alone for a while. But it seemed in a blink of an eye, *I* was about to graduate from the seventh grade, and now it was my business, or at least so I thought.

Daddy picked up trash around the local White high school, and one day when I was his helper, he asked me if I wanted to go to that school. Now it was my time to be shocked, because I knew that school wasn't for Colored children. I also knew that the right answer was, "Sure." When I said, "Sure," Daddy grinned from ear to ear.

I had learned from my many whippings that I couldn't always guess what Daddy was thinking. When he started the process for sending me to that school for Whites only, all I could think about was at last I was going to be Daddy's little girl again.

I ended up making history by going to that high school. It was not the happy adventure that I thought it would be.

PHOEBE: When I was born, Baltimore was about one-quarter African American, but by the time I left for college in 1970, the percentage had risen to 50%. What happened? White flight. When an African American family moved into a White neighborhood, the realtors convinced the White families that they better sell, because their property values were going to plummet. They moved out of the city. But that did not happen in my neighborhood and other more prosperous neighborhoods like it. They remained enclaves of Whiteness. All my neighbors were White, as were my church and my school.

Obviously, there was plenty of racism in Baltimore when I lived there, but I did not have concerns about it when I was young. I didn't think about it. I just thought it was normal for White people to live in some neighborhoods and Black people to live in other neighborhoods. White people had better houses, better stuff, and more money. That's just how it was.

I began to get an inkling that something was really wrong when I was 15, and Dr. Martin Luther King, Jr. was murdered. There were big riots in Baltimore. I could see that on TV. But what I could not figure out was why the Black people were looting and burning their own neighborhoods. By this time, I had heard about the Civil Rights Movement and knew that Black people were no longer willing to accept dilapidated housing, low paying jobs, and poor schools. I knew that they were mad at us, so why did they not come after *us*? Don't get me wrong, I did not want them to come after us. But why were they hurting themselves? What I did not know was that they were mostly destroying the White businesses in their neighborhoods.

By 2007, Phoebe's and Betty's perspectives on life had changed. They had grown up, but they were still learning.

PHOEBE: I knew that I had lived a privileged life, though I was not totally aware of the extent of my White privilege and of my and my family's role in the oppression of Black people. I had recently discovered that my family had enslaved people prior to the end of the Civil War. I thought that Betty might be a descendant of those persons, and I felt compelled to find out if that was true.

BETTY: At this point, Daddy had gone home to be with the Lord. I had become the warrior that he was and that I wanted to be. I fought and I got my education, beginning with an Associate's degree, eventually earning a Master's degree, and then being awarded an honorary Doctor of Humane Letters. Daddy died before I became Dr. Betty Kilby Fisher Baldwin. I wanted to hang up my war shoes and study war no more. Then I met Phoebe Kilby.

This is the story of how Betty and Phoebe met, what they made of each other, and how they are discovering more connections between them than a girl from Happy Creek, Virginia, and a girl from Baltimore, Maryland, could have believed possible.

A CHILD'S POINT OF VIEW

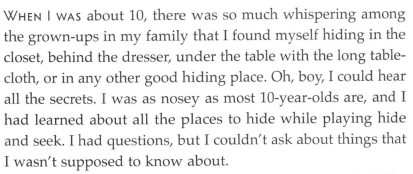

BETTY

WHEN I WAS about 10, there was so much whispering among the grown-ups in my family that I found myself hiding in the closet, behind the dresser, under the table with the long table-cloth, or in any other good hiding place. Oh, boy, I could hear all the secrets. I was as nosey as most 10-year-olds are, and I had learned about all the places to hide while playing hide and seek. I had questions, but I couldn't ask about things that I wasn't supposed to know about.

After church on Sunday we visited family in Peola Mills. When we visited Granddaddy John, we didn't stay long. That was okay with me because there were no children my age and there was no food. Our second stop was about a mile down the road at my great-uncle Sims's. His daughter Mary, her husband, and their children all lived together in that big house. There was no hiding and listening here, because there were plenty of children and some of my favorite foods.

The children played outside while the adults visited inside, and the women all helped with the cooking. We were playing a game where we sang "Up the green mountain, down the green hill, the last one squat must tell their will." This meant that if you were the last to squat, you had to tell a secret.

I had gotten caught so many times that I was running out of secrets. I began to sing, "Old Man Dick Finks stole Daddy's land, Old Man Dick Finks stole Daddy's land, Old Man Dick Finks stole Daddy's land." As I began to sing my fourth stanza, I saw Daddy running toward me with his tongue rolled. He would fold his tongue in his mouth, so that it looked like he had a top, middle, and bottom lip. You could see the underside of

Betty Kilby with her father, James W. Kilby, & mother, Catherine Kilby, in 1958.

his tongue, with the veins in his forehead protruding, so that he looked like a monster. He whipped me all the way to the car. With each lick, he said one word at a time, "Telling...tales... young...lady...well...I... will...teach...you.... Get...in...the... car...and...stay...there...until...I...am...ready...to...leave."

I was heartbroken and crying uncontrollably. I couldn't understand what I did wrong. After all, it was just a game. I could imagine Momma, Daddy, and my brothers eating fried chicken, corn pudding, string beans, potato salad, sweet potatoes, rolls, and cake with the icing so thin you could see the cake. I just couldn't understand what I did to deserve such a punishment.

Oh, man, when everyone came to the car, I wasn't allowed to get all the hugs and love from my cousins, and Daddy wouldn't let anybody bring me food. I didn't know which hurt the most—no food or no love. When we got home, I was instructed to go straight to my room.

One day I heard Daddy dictating a letter to my brother Jimmy. Daddy said "Help! Old Man Dick Finks stole my land when I as a black man had a deed to the property." Daddy told Jimmy, "Pay attention boy, did you get that?" Jimmy said, "Yes, Sir." I was really confused. Daddy was unmerciful in punishing me for repeating the same thing.

When Jimmy put the letter and the big document in the envelope, licked the seal, put stamps on it, placed it in the mailbox, and raised the red flag, I went to see who it was addressed to. J. Edgar Hoover. I still didn't understand.

I saw Jimmy put something under the seat of Daddy's car. I got it and took it to my secret hiding place. If Daddy missed it, he would think Jimmy forgot to put it back under the seat.

Neither Jimmy nor I got caught. I read it as quick as I could. I was still confused because it read

VIRGINIA; IN THE CIRCUIT COURT OF RAPPAHANNOCK COUNTY!

JOHN HENRY KILBY COMPLAINANT v. JAMES WILSON KILBY AND CATHERINE AUSBERRY KILBY DEFENDANTS

Rappahannock County Court House
Washington, Virginia
Wednesday July 13, 1955

It was my granddaddy Kilby who was taking my daddy to court. It took several days of hiding under the table before I learned why.

Daddy grew up on the Finks farm. He was only allowed to go to school through third grade. Then he had to quit school to work on the farm. He had learned in school that slavery was over, but he didn't receive any pay for his work.

By the time he was 17, he threatened to leave the farm. Shortly thereafter, Finks and Daddy's mother gave my daddy the deed to 24 acres of land. His mother told him to put the deed away in a safe place because it was very important—it showed that he owned the land.

Now, 18 years later, Granddaddy comes to visit and asks for the land back. Daddy told Momma that Old Man Dick Finks put Granddaddy up to going to court.

When Daddy and Momma went to court, Momma's niece Fee came to stay with us children. In just one day, the all-white jury ruled in Granddaddy's favor. The land went back to Granddaddy, and Granddaddy turned it over to Old Man Dick Finks. Daddy told Momma that he felt betrayed by his own father. He said that if we didn't get a good education, we would be taken advantage of, and we, too, would have this incredible feeling of hopelessness and despair.

Now it was all coming back to me! I remembered the day when I was playing in the field, and I saw Daddy crying like people do at funerals when they've lost a loved one. That was the day it happened.

———

Once our house was broken into and the intruder took my favorite doll, and I remember being upset at the intruder. I figured I must have deserved that punishment for telling Daddy's secret when I was playing that game long ago.

Whenever Daddy prayed for *everybody,* including Old Man Dick Finks during family prayer, I made sure that I didn't hold Daddy's hand because I wasn't going to pray for Old Man Dick Finks, and I wasn't going to pray for the intruder who stole my doll, and I didn't want to get punished for not participating in the prayer.

For some reason that I didn't know or understand, we stopped visiting Granddaddy John until he got sick, and Daddy visited him one school night. The next day we got word that they found Granddaddy John in the field with his hands still wrapped around the cow's udders. Momma had answered the phone and was the first to receive the message. She told Daddy. Daddy was so upset. He said, "Old Man Dick Finks worked my momma to death and now he has worked my daddy to death. When will the misery ever end?"

But that wasn't the end of trouble. The next day, Momma's niece Fee was lighting her stove. She poured kerosene in the stove, not knowing that there were embers, and the stove blew up, and Fee caught on fire. She ran outside, and one of her four children was holding on to her dress tail. Fee was pregnant at the time. They delivered the baby, and even the baby's lips, toes, and fingers were burned. They both died. The little boy who held onto her dress tail survived.

There was so much sadness around the house that week. We went to Fee's house to sit with her family. We saw the burned bush where Fee fell on the ground, along with an outline of her body where she fell and burned. Surely that must have been some kind of sign from God. On the few occasions when Momma and Daddy left us, Fee was our babysitter. She was the kindest, most gentle person that I ever met. We all loved her.

Now Granddaddy is gone, Daddy's land is gone—and Fee is gone, too.

———•———

We couldn't stay in hotels at that time because African Americans weren't allowed. Hotels were segregated, and there were no African American-owned hotels nearby. Daddy's baby brother John came for Granddaddy's funeral, and he stayed with us. Uncle John was in the military, and he looked so good in his uniform. He could fight for our country, but there were still places he couldn't go. I didn't mind so much because we hadn't seen him in a long time, and Daddy seemed so happy to be with his little brother.

Old Man Dick Finks came to Granddaddy's funeral. He sat right next to Daddy's brother Charles with the family at the funeral. I kept my eyes on my daddy because I didn't know what to expect. He was a broken man, but he said, "Good morning, Mr. Finks." Old Man Dick Finks reached out and shook Daddy's hand and said, "Your father was a good man." That surprised me. I wanted to kick him and say, "You worked my grandfather to death," but I didn't. I wasn't going to speak to him nice and polite either.

———•———

The cemetery was across the road from the church. After the service, they rolled the body across the street and put it in the ground. Old Man Dick Finks and my Uncle Charles left together. Everyone else went back to the church to eat and visit. I couldn't wait to play with my cousins and eat some good food. No one was watching to see how many desserts I was eating, so I got my fill. I must have sampled all the desserts.

The ride home was quiet. Uncle John was coming back to the house, so we were given marching orders for when we got home. I changed my clothes and went downstairs and got under the big dining room table. Daddy and Uncle John sat at the table, but they didn't know how near I was.

My daddy was "Wilson" to most of his immediate family. Uncle John asked, "Wilson, how could you look at Finks and speak so nice and politely after all he has done to you?"

Daddy said, "You know, we were in God's house, and God commands us to love one another. I have to love him, but the sorry things that he has done? I will fight them with all my might."

Uncle John asked, "Well, did you forgive Daddy for taking you to court and getting those 24 acres of land that our momma gave you the deed to?"

Daddy said, "I didn't have to forgive Daddy, because Old Man Dick Finks made him do that, and I know it. Daddy turned around and gave the land back to Finks. That hurt real bad that our daddy was so deeply rooted with that slave mentality that he would betray his own family for Finks. He had to live with that."

Uncle John said, "Well, Charles hasn't changed a bit. He is stuck right up under Finks."

Daddy said, "Man, I tell you. I am so glad we got away from that place. Old Man Dick Finks tried to take our very souls and everything we had. Yes, he got my land, and he got mad when he couldn't get my soul. I probably should thank him because I am going to do everything in my power to make sure that my children get a good education. The best revenge is to succeed in spite of."

I fell asleep under the table. I woke up cold and in the dark. I went upstairs and went to bed.

The next day was Fee's funeral. That one was heartbreaking. The infant was buried in the casket with her mom. Fee was so young and so beautiful. Her two little girls were so cute. I wished we could have adopted them, but that was not to be. Their grandmother and father would have to raise them.

The preacher quoted from Isaiah 40:30-31. He said, "Even youth grow tired and weary and young men stumble and fall, but those that hope in the Lord will renew their strength. They will soar on wings like eagles; they will run and not grow weary; they will walk and not faint." So much hurt, so much pain. Tomorrow will be better.

The next day was better. Uncle John went back to his military duties. The boys got their bed back. Daddy went back to work. As for me, I was still a child hiding under the table eavesdropping, full of curiosity, still playing in the fields and learning from my mistakes. Momma oftentimes said I was as wild as a rabbit.

WAR IS NOT THE ANSWER

3

PHOEBE

BEFORE WE KNEW it, still reeling from the horror of the September 11 attacks, we were at war with Afghanistan. President George W. Bush launched Operation Enduring Freedom to pursue al Qaeda less than a month later, on October 7, 2001.

At the time I was not sure what to think, but responding to the attack with another attack so quickly seemed foolhardy. Did we really know who was responsible? Did we know why they would do such a thing? What might we have done to them to cause this? Responding to violence with more violence—wasn't that just lowering ourselves to the terrorists' level?

But it was a very fearful time, the fears heightened by anthrax attacks, the shoe bomber, and the sniper shootings in the Washington D.C. area. I lived outside D.C. and often did consulting work and shopped there. I remember going with my husband and stepson to a big-box store in the D.C. suburbs and looking around fearfully, wanting to get in and out as quickly as possible. No one knew who the snipers were. Were they another al Qaeda cell?

By early 2003, my questions about the morality and wisdom of war were growing. At the same time, the Bush Administration was making their case that the U.S. should initiate war in Iraq as well. The evidence seemed flimsy to me. I had missed my chance to protest the war in Afghanistan. I decided that I could not stand by as the U.S. contemplated war with Iraq.

I called my college friend Wendy, and we agreed to join the January 18, 2003 march sponsored by A.N.S.W.E.R. Over 500,000 people were on the Mall to "Stop the War Before It Starts." But the next day, the news media accounts seemed to dismiss the movement.

Wendy and I decided to continue our protests and joined the Code Pink March

Phoebe's friend Wendy Blouin Harmic at the A.N.S.W.E.R. March for Peace, January 18, 2003.

on International Woman's Day, March 8, 2003. She brought along her young son in a stroller and carried a sign saying, "Soldiers are somebody's children." My sign had a drawing of a tree with the names "Martin," "Rosa," "Gandhi," and "Dalai Lama" on each of the roots, and the words, "Growing Peace," among the branches and leaves.

Though we were marching in protest of potential actions of our government, we did not feel unsafe, even walking past the armed police with their batons, pistols, and bullet-proof shields in view. Just the fact that Wendy felt she could bring her son showed that we did not march in fear. (What a difference between these marches in 2003 and what we see in 2020 and 2021.)

Code Pink March for Peace & Justice, March 8, 2003.

It struck me that it was pretty easy work, this peace-marching. It felt in some ways more like a festival than a protest march. The speakers at the Ellipse were inspiring and made excellent points, but was anyone in the White House listening? The U.S. entered the Iraq War 12 days later, on March 20.

Meanwhile, my life continued as it had before. My consulting firm offered services in urban and environmental planning and had several contracts with local, state, and the Federal governments. I was currently working for the City of Harrisonburg, Virginia, on their City Comprehensive Plan. As part of this planning effort, it was my job to hold public hearings on what the citizens wanted for the future of their city's growth and development. I also interviewed major institutions in town to learn about their growth plans, including the two universities.

As I sat in the waiting room of the Vice President of Eastern Mennonite University (EMU) waiting for my interview,

I picked up a copy of the college catalog from the coffee table. When I flipped through it, I noticed that there were courses in Peacebuilding, Conflict Transformation, and Restorative Justice. I had never heard of courses like these being offered in college. I made a note to come back later and inquire about them. Obviously, those peace marches had not done anything to keep the U.S. from going to war. Perhaps I could learn from these courses how to be more effective at promoting peace.

Within a week or two, I had an appointment with Ruth Zimmerman, Executive Director of the Conflict Transformation Program (now the Center for Justice and Peacebuilding [CJP]) at EMU. She explained that CTP (CJP) was a graduate program offering a master's degree in Conflict Transformation. She reviewed the kinds of courses I could take, and I was sold. But she suggested that before I sign up, I try a course at the school's Summer Peacebuilding Institute (SPI), where the classes are concentrated into seven day-long sessions.

I signed up for a beginning class, Conflict Analysis, with Dr. Jayne Docherty, and challenged myself by taking it for credit toward a degree, rather than just as a training class. This would require me to write papers afterwards, something I had not done since I had gotten my Master's degree in Environmental Management in 1976. But if I was serious about peacebuilding, I felt I should commit myself.

I loved the class. It was filled with people from all over the world, many from conflict hot spots, all dedicated to working for peace in their countries. We learned how to analyze a conflict so that we could select and develop best practices to address that conflict. We explored such questions as: Who are the parties to this conflict? What are their positions, and what do they say they are fighting for or against? What is the history of the conflict, its origins, its progression, the length of time it has been going on? Who has power, and what kinds of power? What role does identity (nationality, religion, gender, etc.) play? What are the cultural differences? What stories are the parties to the conflict telling about themselves, their opponents, and the conflict? How do these stories reflect their biases and worldviews?

I learned that conflict analysis also involves self-analysis to understand the factors that affect my own personal response to conflict.

When I think about this now, many years later, I see that I was starting to ask some of these questions in a naïve way when I questioned the wars in Afghanistan and Iraq. I just had a very incomplete understanding and no language or tools, not to mention information, to analyze those conflicts before taking this class.

It turns out that our own U.S. government jumped into the war in Afghanistan and continued it without many of the answers to these questions. "We were devoid of a fundamental understanding of Afghanistan—we didn't know what we were doing," Douglas Lute, a three-star Army general who served as the White House's Afghan war czar during the Bush and Obama administrations, told government interviewers in 2015. So those of us who questioned this war, and the war in Iraq, were not so wrong to be protesting back in 2002 and 2003.

Another important lesson I learned is that there are many types of conflict. Conflict may be violent or nonviolent. It can occur at personal, family, community, national, and international levels. There can be systemic conflicts, such as systems of oppression and domination. As it turns out, it is these that I would end up dedicating my peacebuilding efforts to.

In the fall of 2003, I was accepted into the Conflict Transformation Program (Center for Justice and Peacebuilding) to pursue a Graduate Certificate in Conflict Transformation part-time. I joined a group of about 25 persons, several of them Fulbright Scholars. They came from Nigeria, Kenya, Uganda, India, Pakistan, Nepal, Myanmar, Sri Lanka, Croatia, Bosnia-Herzegovina, and Italy, as well as Canada and the United States. In later sessions, we were joined by a whole Middle East contingent from Israel, Palestine, Lebanon, and Syria.

———•———

My first semester class was "Practice: Skills for Conflict Transformation." One experience from this class that sticks with me most is the initial exercise designed to help us learn about ourselves and each other through a day-long ropes course.

We met outdoors at a camp and retreat center set in the woods in rural Rockingham County, Virginia. First, we had to work together to meet a simple, yet challenging goal. All of us were directed to stand on a low wooden platform set about one foot above the ground. There was barely enough room for all of us to stand on this platform. About 10 feet away was another platform of the same size and height. Our goal was to get all of us from one platform to the other without anyone touching the ground. The other platform was too far away for any one of us to jump to it.

We had two eight-foot by eight-inch boards to use, neither long enough to extend from one platform to the other. We could use these any way we wanted, but neither of the boards could ever touch the ground.

Quickly, one of our group took charge, Ashok from India. He solicited ideas with intense enthusiasm and then made proposals. Finally, we came up with a scheme where as many of the heaviest of us as possible stood on one end of the board, and we slid the other board out over the top of the stable board until its end laid on top of the other platform. We sent the lightest of us out over the boards, Jenny from Pakistan. She made it to the other side. We did this one by one, until the last person was left on the first platform. But then we figured out how to get him over, too.

———

Cheers and high fives broke out! We had done it! People from different countries and different cultures, personalities, sizes, and genders, who barely knew each other, had made this happen. We had worked together cooperatively because we all intensely wanted to show that we could do it, and do it without a lot of argument. It seemed like a test of our peace-building aptitude. We had passed!

Next was a more individual challenge, performed one by one. We each had to climb up a web of ropes to a platform. Then we were directed to walk on a wire, while holding on to two higher wires on either side. We were harnessed onto a wire above us so that we could not fall to the ground, but the connection was loose. It was up to each of us to balance; the harness provided no help. Our goal was a much higher plat-form in a tree about 40 feet above the ground. Finally, each of us would be harnessed into a zipline to glide down through the trees to a low platform on the ground.

We were all looking at each other, thinking about who would go first. My inclination was to let some others go first, so I could see how it was done. But then, suddenly, I wanted to go first because I was worried that watching the others would cause me to chicken out. So up I went.

The rope web was not too hard to handle, but walking up the wire was difficult. The wire kept wanting to swing from side to side, making me feel that I would lose my balance. After some shaky steps, I got the hang of it. My classmates started to cheer. Toma from Nigeria was calling me "balance woman" and joining the cheers. To him, I was "balance woman" for the rest of my CJP career. I made it to the high platform, where a staff person strapped me into another harness for the zipline.

I had never done anything like this before. I have never been a fan of scary rides in amusement parks. Looking down from the platform, the view was terrifying. How was I going to step off that platform? It truly felt like a leap of faith, like I was stepping off into nothing. I would put a foot out, then pull it back. It felt like an eternity was going by. My classmates were down below looking at me. And another was heading to my platform where there wasn't much room. I had to go and now.

I stepped off, and down I slid, grasping the harness straps tightly. Terror turned into exhilaration, and I raised my hands and cheered. I felt some pride that day that I had met the challenge and had been the first in our group to do it. What a simple challenge compared to the real ones to come.

———

I learned a great deal from my other CJP classes. I will tell only a few stories which I think about often and which have loomed large in my attempts to become a peacebuilder.

One of my most meaningful classes was Fundamentals of Peacebuilding taught by Dr. John Paul Lederach. He counseled us that since conflict is part of the human condition, thinking that one can permanently resolve it is foolhardy. It's better to look at conflict as an indicator that something is amiss and that change is needed. The goal of conflict transformation is to transform the negative energy of a conflict and to use that energy to build constructive change and to foster reconciliation.

Dr. Lederach developed some of these ideas when working with Conciliation Teams in Nicaragua to address its violent conflicts. The teams often began their meetings with a reading of Psalm 85, verse 10. "Truth and Mercy have met together; Justice and Peace have kissed." What a beautiful way to describe the place where reconciliation is found! To reconcile, conflicting parties must tell the truth and admit to wrongdoings, or else resentment will fester.

Those who have been harmed need to show some mercy after hard truths are told, in order to continue to engage and work toward peace. But peace alone is not adequate. Injustices also must be addressed. As Dr. Lederach listened to these readings of Psalm 85 day by day, he said, "I could hear their voices in the war in Nicaragua. In fact, I could hear their voices in any conflict. Truth, mercy, justice, and peace were no longer just ideas. They became people, and they could talk." (Lederach, *Journey Toward Reconciliation*)

We learned to experience these voices. He divided us into four groups, one for Truth, one for Mercy, one for Justice, and one for Peace. Each group received a set of probing questions to discuss. Then each group chose a representative to embody their idea. The fun began as each person made their argument about why they were most important to achieve reconciliation and how they would do it.

How would they know when reconciliation was achieved? How is constructive change made? The need for *all* these persons/voices—Truth, Mercy, Justice, and Peace—became readily apparent. Also apparent was how reconciliation could be lost and conflict reignited. Yet there seemed to be hope that that new conflict could also be transformed.

Conflict is just part of the flow of life, not necessarily all bad, but rather a catalyst for positive change. Ever since this class, I often find myself calling on "Truth, Mercy, Justice, and Peace" for inspiration.

Mercy, Truth, Justice and Peace.

The students I met in class, not just the lessons, were also inspiring. During my second year of classes, the Middle East group joined us. I will never forget them coming into Strategic Negotiation class on the first day. I could feel the tension as four women—one from Israel, one from Palestine, one from Lebanon, and one from Syria—entered the room. Talk about an intractable set of conflicts, where negotiations often falter!

But by the end of the semester, these women were friends. The language of peacebuilding and principled negotiation had provided them the means to talk to each other and to see a way to work out their differences. That did not mean that they agreed on everything. But they saw each other as human beings, interested in achieving some semblance of peace with justice.

One last story—and it gets close to the reason I started this journey. I was in a class called Strategic Nonviolence. One of our resources was the book *Waging Nonviolent Struggle* by Gene

Sharp, which describes 198 methods of nonviolent action. These include protest marches, parades, pilgrimages, sit-ins, boycotts, issuing of statements and positions, walkouts, strikes, vigils, street theater, withholding of financial resources, refusals to pay debts, public speeches, media campaigns, and on and on.

I raised my hand and said, "I participated in many peace marches to protest the war in Iraq. No one seemed to be listening, and the government just went ahead to war anyway. Don't you think that protest marches have seen their day? Shouldn't we just strike them off the list and deem them ineffective?"

Before the instructor could answer, another student raised his hand. "Phoebe, I think you are wrong, and I will tell you why. I am from Pakistan. When the U.S. went to war with Afghanistan, there were many violent protests in Pakistan. People saw the U.S. as a monolithic evil empire bent on destroying Islam. People died in these protests.

"When the U.S. went into Iraq, this extensive violence did not happen again in Pakistan. We had seen your protests on our TV broadcasts. We saw that there were citizens in the U.S. who were trying to prevent their government from going to war with another Islamic country. It was not the monolithic Christian West against the Islamic East. So I believe that your marches in Washington reduced violence in Pakistan. You never know who you might reach with these kinds of nonviolent actions." I have kept that amazing story with me all these years.

I graduated from the Center for Justice and Peacebuilding in the Fall of 2004, although I continued to audit courses and take Summer Peacebuilding Institute classes so I could keep on learning. CJP also involved me in a few special projects, the most notable being the Women's Peacebuilding Leadership Program. They assembled a group of women peacebuilders from around the world to develop the parameters for the project. I was honored to serve with these powerful women, including Leymah Gbowee, who later was awarded the Nobel Peace Prize in 2011 for her work in Liberia.

But what to do with this degree? I was a 52-year-old woman in the U.S. with no international experience and a life very grounded with my husband in Virginia. I could not go abroad as a number of my classmates did to work for peace-building NGOs. Besides, I didn't think I would have the moral authority to help people in other cultures work for peace. I am an American, and I know my culture best, or at least I thought I did when it comes to making positive change. But I was at a loss about where exactly I fit in.

Meanwhile, I figured I would apply my peacebuilding skills to all those planning and zoning conflicts I encountered in my planning consultancy. I would have to bide my time until my true calling surfaced.

CJP Women's Peacebuilding Leadership Program Planning Team. Rear from left: Warigia Hinga (Kenya), Dekha Abdi (Kenya), Koila Costello-Olsson (Fiji), Phoebe Kilby (US), Alma Jadallah (US/Middle East), Daria White (Bulgaria/US). Front from left: Elaine Barge (US), Paulette Moore (US), Rubina Bhatti (Pakistan), Lauren Sauer (US), Leymah Gbowee (Liberia), Jan Jenner (US).

SOLDIERS WITHOUT UNIFORMS

4

BETTY

ON THE THIRD Sunday of July 1957, I was baptized in the Jordan River in Flint Hill, Virginia. It was customary at Macedonia Baptist Church to have a week-long revival leading up to a homecoming service and baptism.

We had a snack stand open after the evening revival services that sold candy, sodas, chips, sandwiches, and ice cream. Daddy gave me money to put in the offering—a penny and a quarter. I put the penny in the collection plate and saved the quarter to buy a ZERO candy bar after the service. I loved that candy with its white chocolate coating and caramel, peanuts, and almond nougat.

On our way home, I took a bite. That luscious smell let my brothers and sister know I had candy. They each wanted a piece. They got mad because I wouldn't share, and they told Daddy I had candy. Daddy wanted to know how I got the candy. I told him that I used my church money. He gave me a tongue-lashing you wouldn't believe. He said that I stole from God and I had to repent. I wish he had just beaten me. It would have been better than facing God's wrath.

On Wednesday night, the preacher spoke from Matthew 3: 1-17; his subject, "A Voice in the Wilderness." Because I had to sit with Momma during the rest of the revival, I was paying attention. This was my chance to repent and be forgiven for robbing God. When the preacher gave the invitation to repent and come to Jesus, I got up and went to the front and sat in that big chair. My cousins Carolyn and Demi came up, too. I reminded them after the service that we would be baptized in the Jordan River just like Jesus. I can't say that we were always good godly children after that. In fact, the preacher said that we would need to study the Word and go to Sunday school so we would learn how to be godly children.

Daddy was in relentless pursuit to get us educated. He started a 4-H club in our neighborhood of Happy Creek. He said it would be a good opportunity for the boys to learn and grow. Most of the neighborhood boys joined and were each given a pig to take care of as a project. My brothers Jimmy and John both got pigs.

Daddy even got his picture in the *American Viscose Magazine*. He was working at the factory full-time as a janitor and managing his 52-acre farm. We had about 50 head of milk cows, a bunch of chickens, about 25 hogs, two ducks, and a dog. Daddy said, "The 4-H project will teach the youth responsibility and develop leadership skills." John won first place in the pig-raising contest, and Jimmy got second place.

We didn't need 4-H to teach us responsibility and leadership because Daddy was doing a real good job. The boys were already milking cows before and after school, and I was taking care of the chickens and collecting eggs.

In 1956, my oldest brother Jimmy was about to graduate from Ressie Jeffries Elementary School. Offering only grades one through seven, this was the school that Warren County provided for "Colored children." Daddy had joined the PTA, and then was elected President of the PTA. He knew all our teachers and everything we did at school.

At that time, when African American children graduated from the 7th grade, they were either finished with school and went to work on somebody's farm, or they went to Manassas to the Manassas Regional High School (MRHS).

MRHS was located in another county, about a one-hour drive from Front Royal. It was founded in 1893 through the efforts of former slave Jennie Dean. The school was designed to be a private residential school for African Americans which provided academic and vocational training within a Christian setting. However, in 1937, the public school systems of Fairfax, Fauquier, and Prince William counties took over the school and established it as a public regional school for African American students.

Daddy was real pleased with himself when he announced to Jimmy that he would not need to drop out of school but would be going to Manassas Regional High School when he graduated from Ressie Jeffries. I could tell by Momma's face she wasn't happy, and Jimmy cried. I knew this could not be good. Jimmy didn't like sleepovers; he liked his own bed. John asked, "Who is going to help with the milking?" Daddy said, "Don't worry. Everything is going to be all right."

The day came for Jimmy to go off to high school. We were normal kids. We fought like cats and dogs, but we loved each other. We all cried. We thought Jimmy would be able to come home every weekend, but he was only allowed to come home every two weeks on the bus. We cried and carried on so that Daddy drove the 50 miles to Manassas and picked Jimmy up. Daddy talked to the bus driver and found out there was a vacant seat on the bus returning to the school on Monday morning. The driver let Jimmy ride back on the bus.

The next thing you know, we were picking Jimmy up every other week right after we milked the cows on Friday evening, and Jimmy was riding back to the school on the bus every Monday morning.

Jimmy didn't like the school. The big boys picked on him and took his money because he was younger. One night Jimmy went to the cafeteria to get his midnight snack. The security guard saw him in the cafeteria drinking milk. The guard asked him, "What are you doing, Boy?" Jimmy said that he was getting a midnight snack, but the guard called it stealing. Jimmy lost his bus privilege for stealing.

Jimmy called Daddy to come and get him. Daddy told Jimmy that it was the week for him to come home on the bus. Then Jimmy explained to Daddy about the misunderstanding about the milk. Daddy called the principal about the incident. Daddy thought that as an African American and father, the principal would understand that Jimmy had never been away from home and was innocent enough to think that it was all right for him to go in the refrigerator like he did at home. But there was no reasoning with the man.

The principal told Daddy that he didn't have any rights because he didn't live in the county. Daddy was mad. He called our local school board office. He told them that he didn't understand why Jimmy had to go so far away and stay in a boarding school and that it was costly for him to have to go to Manassas every other weekend. Besides, Jimmy wasn't being protected from the bullies. He told them that he wasn't

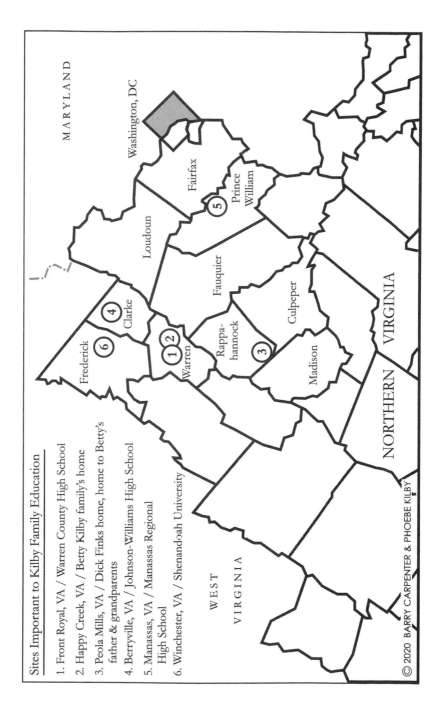

Sites Important to Kilby Family Education

1. Front Royal, VA / Warren County High School

2. Happy Creek, VA / Betty Kilby family's home

3. Peola Mills, VA / Dick Finks home, home to Betty's father & grandparents

4. Berryville, VA / Johnson-Williams High School

5. Manassas, VA / Manassas Regional High School

6. Winchester, VA / Shenandoah University

MARYLAND

Washington, DC

Fairfax

Prince William

Loudoun

Fauquier

Clarke

Culpeper

Frederick

Rappa-hannock

Warren

Madison

WEST VIRGINIA

NORTHERN   VIRGINIA

© 2020 BARRY CARPENTER & PHOEBE KILBY

going to send Jimmy back to Manassas next year and that his son John wasn't going to Manassas either, so they needed to find a better solution.

The next thing we knew, Jimmy was coming home every weekend on the bus.

As John approached graduation from Ressie Jeffries Elementary, Daddy was in constant meetings with the school board. The school board was offering another option for Colored children to get an education beyond elementary school. Daddy was excited about having both boys at Johnson-Williams High School. Jimmy was happy to be living at home once again. John was disappointed that he wasn't going to get time off from milking the cows.

The first day of school in the fall of 1957, Jimmy and John were excited to walk the half-mile from our house to the railroad crossing to board the bus going to Johnson-Williams High School in Berryville, Virginia. Berryville is located in neighboring Clarke County, about a half-hour drive from Front Royal. But it wasn't long before Daddy and the boys were getting tired and weary. The White children would yell racial words from the windows of their bus at Jimmy and John as they walked to the bus stop. One day as they walked to meet the bus for African American students, the bus carrying White students hit a pothole in the road and splashed water on Jimmy and John. They were soaking wet. They considered going back to the house to change, but they would have missed their bus, and that would have resulted in a punishment they didn't want to think about.

The African American school bus broke down far too often, and Daddy was often milking all the cows without help. The day came when the bus broke down completely, and the school board had to send a replacement bus. The children were stuck on the side of the road for hours. There was not a designated Colored bus or driver available. The children had to wait for one of the White drivers to go home and eat his dinner, and then come pick up the Colored children. They didn't get home until after midnight. Jimmy and John still had to get up at 4:00 a.m. to help Daddy milk the cows before he went to work.

The children talked about how nice the bus for the White children was. Daddy complained to the school board and petitioned for a new bus. They got a better bus, a hand-me-down from the White children. Daddy was not happy about his inability to educate his children.

While the boys were at Johnson-Williams, Daddy met and became friends with Reverend Frank, a highly educated Methodist minister and a teacher at Johnson-Williams. Daddy learned all about the 1954 Supreme Court Brown decision, the related court cases in Virginia, and the National Association for the Advancement of Colored People (NAACP).

James Wilson Kilby, Betty's father.

Rev. Frank spoke at the PTA meeting. "It's a good time for Colored folks in America today. Oliver Brown wanted his daughter, Linda Brown, to go to an all-White elementary school in Topeka, Kansas. It wasn't just Oliver Brown; there were five cases from the North in Delaware, from the South in South Carolina, from the East in Virginia, and in Washington D.C. The anti-segregation movement had some smart, powerful lawyers and the backing of the NAACP. All five cases were combined and litigated as Brown v. Board of Education of Topeka. On May 17, 1954, the Supreme Court ruled in favor of ending segregated schools.

"They said segregation in public schools was unconstitutional."

Daddy was so excited, you would have thought he won the lottery. He told Momma, "Oh, Catherine, I have been struggling to figure out how to get these children educated, and I think God has answered my prayers. We are going to have Rev. Frank and his family out to dinner on Sunday. Set the younger children at the table in the kitchen. Betty can watch them. Us grown folks can eat and talk at the dining room table. Make sure there is plenty of food on both tables."

On Sunday, Rev. Frank and his family came to dinner. I loved Rev. Frank's little boys, but those little boys cramped my style. I couldn't hear the adults' conversation. I would have to do Jimmy's and John's chores to get them to tell me all about what the adults said.

Jimmy and John got so excited and talked freely about how these smart African American lawyers had graduated from Howard University and how the two of them were going to go to college and be smart Black men like those lawyers. Daddy got on the phone to organize the NAACP in Warren County. Daddy had Jimmy writing letters, and Daddy was going to the meetings.

Daddy reminded me that I was approaching graduation from 7th grade. He told me that the PTA voted to give the top five students in the graduating class $5 each. If I was in the top five, he would give me $5 also. I listened and learned. The good news about the criteria for being in the top five was that it was based on a standardized test. If I had to depend on being chosen by the teachers, I could have been purposely kept out, because people thought my daddy was a troublemaker. I thought so, too, sometimes, but I loved him. I was among the top five students in my class, and I got my $10. When we took our graduation picture, I held up my two fives in the picture.

I brought my Pupil Placement form home and gave it to Daddy. The form asked where I would attend high school the next year, and it needed a parent's signature. Usually when I brought papers home for him to sign, he would sign and give them right back.

Every day Mrs. Jeffries would ask for my form, and I would ask Daddy. At last, he gave it to me. Mrs. Jeffries called me up front and asked if I scratched on this paper. I said, "No, Ma'am." She said, "Your daddy messed up this form. You tell him all he is supposed to do is circle Johnson-Williams or Manassas, and then sign it and return it to me."

I gave Daddy the form at the dinner table as usual. Then, I gave him the instructions just as Mrs. Jeffries gave them to me. I saw the veins in his forehead puff up, and I knew he was mad. He scratched out Johnson-Williams and Manassas and wrote in Warren County High School again.

He said, "Tell Mrs. Jeffries if she don't like my choice, she should call me." I was scared. Then I got real brave and told Mrs. Jeffries, "If you don't like it you can call my daddy."

She did call Daddy. I answered the phone and handed it to him. I heard him say, "You have my form. My choice is to send Betty to Warren County High School, and you have my signature. All you have to do is send it on to the School Board Office."

The next day Daddy took off work. Daddy, Charlie Dean, Sam Fletcher, John Jackson, and Charles Washington went to Richmond and showed up at Attorney Oliver Hill's office. When they arrived, the secretary asked if they had an appointment, and Daddy said, "No, but I think Mr. Hill will want to talk to us." She left the room and returned. She told them that Mr. Hill was in a meeting and that he would be out in about 30 minutes.

When Mr. Hill came out to greet them, Daddy said, "We are here from the Warren County branch of the NAACP." He introduced each of the men with him and said, "We all have school-age children, and our children are currently going outside the county for a high school education, while the White children are going to school in the county. I want my daughter Betty and our other children to go to Warren County High School. I signed the Pupil Placement form to send Betty to Warren County High School."

Mr. Hill scratched his head and smiled with satisfaction. Then, he said, "You say there is no high school for Colored children in Warren County."

Daddy, growing impatient, asked, "Have you been listening"?

Mr. Hill said, "You know it won't be easy."

Daddy responded, "Ain't nothing been easy up till now, so why should we expect this to be easy?"

Mr. Hill, "Once we get started on this journey, there is no turning back. I have to make some calls, talk to the NAACP home office. You know we have been in litigation in Prince Edward County, Norfolk, Charlottesville, and Arlington, Virginia, for a while now, but you guys are the only ones with no high school for Colored children. You may be what we need to light a fire under these Virginia cases. I need for you to be fully committed, and, I repeat, it won't be easy for you or the children. Call me next week if you still want to go through with the case."

The excitement and tensions were high. We were allowed to attend the NAACP meetings. Daddy gave his report, and then he called for a discussion and the vote. One lady asked if they didn't have children wanting to go to Warren County High School (WCHS), could they vote? The answer: Anyone who was a paid member of the NAACP could vote. Daddy laughed and asked if anyone needed to pay their dues now. Everyone voted yes to move forward with the case. Officials from the national branch of the NAACP attended the meeting, and they said they would meet with Attorney Hill to formulate the next step.

Twenty-four African American children were originally signed up to go to Warren County High School, and five to the White elementary school. Attorney Oliver Hill wrote a letter asking that we all be admitted to the schools. The request was put on the Warren County School Board agenda for August 14, 1958. That meant that I would have to wonder all summer about where I would go to high school in the fall. I was going to have a good summer, because I knew that come fall, it was serious business.

The school board didn't take Attorney Hill's request seriously. At the next NAACP meeting, it was reported that the school

Leaving the strategy session for the School Integration legal case, Attorney Oliver W. Hill at far right. James Wilson Kilby in bow tie at far left.

board went on record saying that there was no room at WCHS for us. The youngest high school student involved was chosen to be named lead plaintiff in the planned court case, just in case it was dragged out for years like the ones filed in 1956 had been.

I was very happy to be chosen as the lead plaintiff. But I soon realized that Betty Ann Kilby et. al. vs. the County School Board of Warren County, Virginia et. al. (Civil Action # 530 August 29, 1958) would put me on the front lines of this war for an education.

On one side, we had powerful, educated, and rich Whites fighting to keep White supremacy. On the other was a handful of poor African American parents relentlessly pursuing an education for their children. They told us plaintiffs that we were soldiers—soldiers in God's army, marching to get an education for all God's children.

Daddy told us to stay away from the cameras and not to talk to reporters, because the only name they were focusing on was Kilby. When we went to Harrisonburg to court, the older children were called to testify. The Kilby children stayed in the background. One of the parents had received a call threatening to kill his children, and he withdrew his children's names.

On September 8, 1958, Federal District Judge John Paul ordered the Warren County School Board to admit the 22 Negroes to the county's only high school. He denied the petition for the elementary school children.

We made our plans for registering for WCHS. We were instructed to answer all the questions on the form and not to leave any blanks. If something didn't require an answer, we were to write "N/A." Each older child partnered up with a younger child.

But after all that preparation, the school board sent us away because they had entered an appeal.

The school board didn't get anywhere with the appeal. On September 11, Judge Simon E. Sabloff of the U.S. Fourth Circuit Court of Appeals refused to grant a stay of the desegregation order. While Attorney Hill was on the road returning to Front Royal, we were preparing to register for school.

On September 12, 1958, Governor Almond closed Warren County High School, the first school closed under the Massive Resistance Laws. Not only did the governor close my school, he closed two schools in Charlottesville and six schools in Norfolk. On that same day, Governor Orval Faubus closed Central High School in Little Rock, Arkansas, the historic school that was integrated by the Little Rock Nine in 1957.

This really messed me up. Now, there were 12,700 children in Virginia locked out of public education. I thought about my cousins going on to high school in Culpeper and Warrenton and my friends going on to high school. But we African American high-schoolers in Warren County were being deprived of an education in an integrated school close to where we lived. I was doomed to be a dummy for the rest of my life, having to work in some White folks' kitchen, being worked to death before I was 60.

The powerful government had it all planned. The Virginia Legislature had put together some laws called the Massive Resistance Laws that allowed the governor to close the schools if any judge ordered compliance with the Brown decision. Attorney Hill tried to console us by telling us the war was not over.

The NAACP organized a group of women from various branches of the NAACP named The Student Committee. We called them our Den Mothers. Their job was to get us ready for the world stage. We girls practiced walking with books on our heads while we sang, "The rain in Spain stays mainly in the plain."

We practiced filling out forms and writing legibly when we did so. We practiced nonviolence and how to act in front of cameras and the media, how to put on a serious yet friendly face. We were being treated like dirt, and we had to pretend to like it.

It was hard for children to be soldiers in this war with no name and no understandable reason. It was hard, too, because we felt bad to see how hard the committee was fighting to keep us safe and emotionally sound.

As White folks were fighting to maintain their way of life, our legal team was fighting for our rights, and our Den Mothers were fighting to protect and care for us children. As Rev. King, as he was known to us, said, "A law or a judicial decree merely declares rights and responsibilities; it doesn't necessarily deliver them. Only when the people themselves began to act are they delivered."

I had to get out of my pity party, but I kept having bad dreams. I was running to catch my bus, but angry White faces were yelling ugly words and throwing rocks at me. I fell. Then I would wake up crying.

The legal team was continuing to fight the Massive Resistance Laws and the school closings. I think they were spending all their time on our case. Meanwhile, our Den Mothers were working to raise money for us to go to integrated schools in Washington, D.C. Our committee was comprised of Colored and White volunteers.

An all-White group who was also raising funds had their White children back in school within days. They were using any available vacant building to hold school with the WCHS teachers, and the White children were riding on taxpayer-paid buses with taxpayer-paid drivers. That didn't last long because our legal team put a stop to the use of public taxpayer money to support private education.

The White folks' donations were coming in by the thousands of dollars, while our funds ranged from one dollar to 100 dollars each. It was December before we were able to get into the integrated schools in D.C. Our committee had dresses made for the girls, and the boys wore suits with light blue shirts to match the embroidered light blue flowers on our pink dresses. We wore them when we went on TV to help raise funds to support us in school. We called our dresses our uniforms; however, we only wore our uniforms at command performances.

On January 19, 1959, the Virginia Supreme Court of Appeals declared that both closing schools and cutting off state funds to prevent racial integration in public schools violated the Virginia Constitution. Oliver Hill was right when he predicted that if he was successful in Front Royal, he would succeed in the other Virginia cases. On February 2, 1959, the case of Clarissa S. Thompson et. al. vs. the School Board of Arlington County Virginia and T. Edward Rutter, Division Superintendent of Arlington, Virginia (Civil Action 1341, May 17, 1956) was won. Arlington, just outside of Washington, D.C., was the first school in Virginia to integrate.

Soon thereafter, integration came as a result of the case of Leola Pearl Beckett et. al. vs. the School Board of the City of Norfolk (Civil Action 2214, May 1956). How interesting that the lead plaintiffs in all of these cases in Virginia were girls.

February 17, 1959, was the night before Warren County High School was to open on an integrated basis. I hated to leave the school in Washington, D.C., but I knew I was a soldier, and I had no choice. Still, it didn't stop my heart from hurting and wanting this to all be over.

I was standing at the kitchen window washing dishes when I heard the blast. Daddy yelled, "Gunfire, hit the floor." I passed out. The dog gave a howl and took off across the field with the doghouse chained to him. I woke to Momma slapping my face and crying hysterically. She thought I had been shot. I was just a scared little girl, and I fainted.

We got ourselves together and went to the planning meeting at Williams Chapel where Rev. Frank was the pastor. We were taught to hold back our tears in public, because we didn't want to show the enemy our fears. I sat in a corner of the church. As Daddy told the group about the shots being fired at our house, tears rolled down my cheeks. Rev. Frank began to pray, and we began to sing. I wasn't afraid anymore, so I moved over and sat with the children. We talked about what time to be ready in the morning and who would ride with whom.

Most of our fathers worked at the American Viscose plant, and they couldn't get off work. It was the women from our committee who drove us to school that morning. Momma didn't drive; she would not be with us as we journeyed to school. I expected a pep talk from our Den Mothers, but everyone was silent.

On February 18, 1959, as we approached WCHS, the police were directing traffic. Mrs. Butler drove Jimmy, John, and me to school because she lived up the road from us. She was instructed to let us out at the bottom of the hill. It took a while for me to gather my thoughts and my body and to get out of the car. I didn't want anybody to think I was scared, so I finally jumped out of the car. As I passed a big fat White woman, she yelled, "We gonna kill all you little Niggas." I was so scared

Integration of Warren County High School, February 18, 1959.

I urinated on myself. Then I began to pray, "The Lord is my Shepherd... Yea, though I walk through the valley of the shadow of death I will fear no evil." At that point, all my Sunday School training kicked in, and I became a mighty warrior. Someone ahead of me began to sing, "We shall overcome." We all became the warriors that we had been training to become.

Not a single White student showed up for school.

The next day we rode the bus, and the driver dropped us off in the rear of the school. Here we were, now 21 students and 15 teachers in a facility that once housed over a thousand students. (Joyce Henderson and Elizabeth Dean were about to graduate with trades that

James and Betty on School Integration Day, February 18, 1959.

were not offered at WCHS, so they did not return the second day.) The White teachers were no more accustomed to teaching little Colored students than we were accustomed to taking instruction from White teachers. That evening on the bus, we were singing, "We bad, we know we bad."

We were pleased that Attorney Hill came through on his promise, and that, at last, we were back in school. I personally felt relieved from the threatening phone calls, at least during the day. I knew the night riders couldn't get into the school, and besides there were lots of places to hide.

Integration of Warren County High School, February 18, 1959.

As we approached the end of the 1958-59 school year, our only African American senior was Ann Rhodes. She needed a half-credit to graduate. Most of us attended summer school to make up that half-credit. When Ann completed the requirements, the school didn't host a graduation, nor did they give her a diploma. The fact is, Ann was the only public high school graduate in Warren County during the 1958-59 school year.

Our Den Mothers had money left over from our time in D.C. They decided that since the school board wouldn't honor Ann, their committee would. They chartered a bus to take us to Atlantic City, New Jersey.

Most of us hadn't ventured far outside of Front Royal, Virginia. Now here we were, headed to Atlantic City, New Jersey! It was a grand adventure to see the Atlantic Ocean and the Boardwalk. We were deemed heroes, but I knew I wasn't a hero because I was afraid and cried all the time, but I was getting better.

The main event on Saturday was wonderful. We wore our pink and blue uniforms. I had no rhythm, and I couldn't dance to the beat of the music, but I closed my eyes and pretended to be Cinderella. We were interviewed on TV and were honored at many functions. I met Rev. King and Thurgood Marshall, and they thought we were heroes, too. Even with summer school, that summer was as good as the summer before was bad.

The summer ended way too soon. About 500 White students returned to Warren County High School. Our safe place soon became the most dangerous place. The County had built Criser School in an effort to prevent WCHS from being integrated. This new combined elementary and high school for Colored children was completed, fully staffed, and in operation that fall.

Our area had two buses that intersected at Criser School. The one let off the children going to Criser. The children going to WCHS boarded the second bus, driven by Bo Flynn for WCHS. The younger Kilby children went to Criser, while the older Kilby children were still soldiers going to WCHS.

Attorney Hill reminded us from the beginning that there was no turning back for us. We were called names by the Colored children, because many thought we weren't coming to Criser because we thought we were too good to go there. We got to WCHS, and the White children were of the mindset that we had a Colored school and we should go to that school. We learned quickly that we didn't fit in anywhere, and that was the way it was.

We made our plans on the bus every day on our way to WCHS from Criser. We checked each other's schedules and tried to pair up as we moved to and from classes because it wasn't safe if we got caught in the halls alone. We had check-in at lunch time to make sure everyone was all right. We pointed out the really bad kids, the ones who would kill you just soon as look at you.

Bo the bus driver would drive really slowly if we needed more time to plan. He was as much a part of our team as our fellow students. He understood our circumstances.

Our nonviolence training allowed us to endure the name-calling and the spitballs that were a daily part of our school life. The constant isolation could have been a good thing, but it hurt when you knew that people held you in such contempt that they acted like we weren't there. Being barred from every good thing like school clubs, sports, and our prom was almost unbearable. One African American girl got married over the Christmas holiday and dropped out, leaving my brother Jimmy and Frank Grier to be the first to graduate as part of an integrated class.

The 1960-61 school year produced WCHS's first integrated class. Again, it was up to our Den Mothers to provide the graduation party and prom for our seniors. They saw that we had a class picture and a formal graduation.

The day after their graduation, two White boys rode their bicycles up the road in front of our house. My little brother Gene was in the front yard playing by himself under the tree. The boys stopped and got off their bicycles, all the time calling Gene names. Gene ran in the house and told us what happened. We forgot all about our nonviolence training because we were "evenly matched" (Ha! Ha!)—five of us (my brother

John, a neighbor friend, Gene, Patty, and me) and two of them. Besides, they started this battle.

We got our mud balls ready for when they came back down the road. We gave Gene instructions to dare them to come into the yard for a fair fight. They got off their bikes and chased Gene into the yard where we were waiting for them with mud balls. We blasted them, and they ran to their bicycles.

What we didn't anticipate is that they would go to the police and say that *Jimmy* and Frank threw rocks at them— accusing Jimmy because they were upset that he had graduated from the integrated high school. That night, policemen showed up at our house with a warrant for James Kilby.

Daddy went to the door to greet the policeman. He said, "I am James Kilby."

The policeman said, "We want your boy."

Daddy said, "My boy is a minor, and your warrant calls for a man, so take me." He was up in their faces and he wasn't afraid.

As the police were pushing Daddy into the car, Daddy told Momma to call Rev. Frank. We told Momma what we did. Momma told Jimmy to go hide in the field until we could get this mess straightened out. Then she called Rev. Frank and told him what happened.

By the time Rev. Frank got to the jail, the police had arrested Frank Grier also. Rev. Frank called our lawyer Otto Tucker. The charges were dropped against both Daddy and Frank Grier. But they issued a juvenile warrant for Jimmy. Daddy, Attorney Tucker, and Rev. Frank accompanied Jimmy to jail. Jimmy pleaded not guilty to assault and battery; however, he was found guilty and was ordered to pay a $50 fine.

Attorney Tucker suggested that Jimmy would be subpoenaed to testify against his brother John. Jimmy was not home at the time of the rock-throwing incident, but he knew that the rock-throwing boys thought John's friend was him. We did not want to get John's friend in trouble. It was difficult enough for the Kilby children to have friends. We didn't want to scare any of them away because they'd fear they could be targeted to testify or thrown in jail, too.

Daddy figured that if Jimmy was not around, he couldn't be subpoenaed. So he packed Jimmy up and took him to D.C. The police came several times, and we told them that Jimmy didn't live here anymore. They watched the house for weeks.

When my brother John got ready to enter his final year in high school, the school board tried to use the rock-throwing incident against him and not let him go to school. Attorney Tucker wouldn't let that happen as long as the police couldn't subpoena Jimmy. Jimmy couldn't join the military because of his record, and he couldn't come back to Warren County, so we visited him in D.C.

One of the white boys involved in the rock-throwing incident, Jim Hamilton, made me pay double. He called me names and threw spitballs at me for the next two years, and I had to practice nonviolence. Our leaders were right; the consequences were harsh if we made mistakes and didn't follow the rules.

My brother John was a unique young man. He could make As and Bs despite the hellish environment that we were exposed to on a daily basis. John and Daddy milked the cows every morning and evening. Two milking machines made milking much faster and easier.

The charges against John were eventually dropped due to lack of evidence. He took the test for the United Negro Scholarship Fund and got a scholarship. He was admitted to Fisk University, where he also got a football scholarship, even though he never played football while in high school, or just for fun. He was incredibly talented both academically and athletically. John graduated in the 1961-62 school year, and the NAACP Student Committee threw the party.

Our mothers lost their domestic jobs, doing washing, ironing, and housecleaning, because of our desegregation case. So they sought employment 70 miles away near Washington D.C. We referred to this area as "down in the country."

When I finished summer school after my junior year, Momma let me go to work with her down in the country. Momma bought two nine-passenger station wagons, hired two drivers, and bused people to work down in the country where the pay was far greater than in Front Royal. I was cleaning white folks' houses. I was getting my money ready, because I was already looking forward to my graduation and my graduation party. The woman I worked for gave me a bunch of hand-me-down clothes, among them a beautiful black lace dress. It fit perfectly, and I could see myself in that dress for my graduation party.

When September of 1962 finally came, I entered my senior year. There was only a handful of us on the bus from Criser to Warren County High School. Our numbers were so small that planning how we were going to partner up for protection was impossible. The ride was so quiet, you could hear a pin fall. Rev. Frank had moved to Philadelphia over the summer. I was thinking, "Lord how are we going to make it through?" A faint small voice inside of me said, "You know I will be with you."

I perked up and said, "Are we ready to graduate? Anybody thinking about college?" Steve Travis, who had an illness that kept him back for a year, said, "I just want to make it through to finish high school without any more sickness." We arrived at WCHS, but I was already starting to count down the days. Pumping myself up in the mornings got harder and harder.

I applied to five Colored colleges—Virginia State, Norfolk State, Virginia Union, Fisk, and Hampton Institute. I thought surely I would get into Hampton Institute. That's where we met Rev. King and Thurgood Marshall, when they were honoring us for bringing about the first desegregation of the schools in Virginia. I didn't get accepted anywhere. When I got real with myself, I realized my grades were so bad that college was out of my future.

After getting detention for being late for class, I just stopped taking all the safety measures we had agreed on as Colored students in an integrated high school. There were too few of us to partner up anymore. One day as I was taking the short cut through the auditorium, I was grabbed and raped. When that happened, I wanted my life to be over. To end.

My Sunday School training told me I couldn't commit suicide because my soul would be in eternal hell. But my life was an eternal hell, and I couldn't do anything about it. Rev. Frank was gone. There was no one to talk to. Every time we broke the rules, the consequences were harsh.

When the builders built our house, they didn't firmly nail one of the panels in my closet. I could pull the panel out and hide behind the wall. It became my secret hiding place. I sat in my safe place crying and wondering where God was when those boys pulled me behind the stage. I had to take responsibility for taking the short cut. I was a soldier, a soldier in God's army marching to get an education for all God's children. It was hard to keep the nonviolence rule in my head. I was explosive.

One day in English class, a boy in the back bombarded me with spitballs. I yelled out in class, "Ms. Czarniski, will you please stop those boys from throwing spitballs at me." I got detention for disrupting the class. They had to clean up the spitballs, and they got detention, too.

On another day, one of the Kersey twins balled up a sheet of notebook paper and threw it at me. It hit me on the head. I picked up the paper and walked over to the girl's desk like a zombie. I placed my hand on her neck and stuffed the paper in her mouth. I could hear Rev. Frank's voice in my head saying, "Betty, always ask yourself, are you willing to face the consequences of your actions." I let go of her neck, walked back over to my desk, and sat down. When the teacher arrived back in the class, there was not a sound to be heard.

I had taken up street racing with the hope of wrecking the car and dying in an accident. I tried just closing my eyes and drifting away. I wasn't eating, and I wasn't sleeping. I ended up in the hospital. The doctors said I was having a nervous breakdown.

One night an orderly, a man from our church, came into my room and sat on my bed. He asked, "What's wrong with you, child"? I answered, "I want to die." He responded, "Me, too." I was shocked at his response. Before I could say anything, he asked, "How long you been in that school"? I replied, "Five years. I graduate in June." He said, "God gave you a big job. You did good. It's almost over. The best part of your life is just ahead of you." I believed him. As easy as he came into my room, he left.

I was released from the hospital. I went back to school believing that God works in mysterious ways. My soul would heal from the deep wounds inflicted by those boys who raped me. I graduated. I wore that black lace dress under my graduating gown. The zipper broke. While waiting for Daddy to bring me another dress, I watched my White classmates hugging and wishing each other success. They still pretended that I wasn't there right up to the bitter end.

Every school year after WCHS was integrated, the school board would let any African American student transfer to WCHS who wanted to. Jerome Jackson was not a plaintiff in our case. He had come in the 1960-61 school year and graduated with us. Barbara Jackson, Steve Travis, Matthew Pines, and I were the last of the infant plaintiffs in the case of Betty Ann Kilby et. al. vs. the County School Board of Warren County Virginia et. al. (Civil Action 530 August 29, 1958).

On February 18, 1958, 23 courageous African American students fulfilled the court order to integrate Warren County High School. We were soldiers in a war to get an education for all God's children. We had made the difference: Betty Ann Kilby, John F. Kilby, James M. Kilby, Gwendolyn Baltimore, John Jackson, Barbara Jackson, Delores Coleman, Faye Coleman, Mary Coleman, Rebecca Fletcher, Louise Dean, Suetta Dean, Elizabeth Mae Dean, Charles Lewis, Archie Pines, Matthew Pines, Ann Rhodes, Dorothy Rhodes, Geraldine Rhodes, Cuetta Grier, Frank Grier, Stephen Travis, and Joyce Henderson.

FAMILY SECRETS

PHOEBE

IN THE SUMMER of 2006, I was taking another class at the CJP's Summer Peacebuilding Institute. One of my former class-mates, Bonnie Lofton, who was CJP's fundraiser, asked me to lunch. Okay, I thought, she's going to ask me for a donation. But no. She told me that she was going to switch jobs at the college and wondered if I would be interested in becoming CJP's fundraiser.

I was totally taken aback and laughed off the idea. I told her I was not interested. But over the next few days, I thought about it. I had been a professional planner for almost 30 years and was getting tired of the work. And besides, I still hadn't found a place for myself as a peacebuilder. Maybe if I made this big change in my life and aligned myself more with CJP, I would be able to find my calling. I applied and was hired in August 2006.

Soon after I arrived on campus, I heard about a program that had started a few months earlier, in January 2006, called Coming to the Table (CTTT). At the request of EMU employee

Will Hairston, CJP convened a gathering of about 25 descendants of enslavers and descendants of persons who were enslaved. Will Hairston's family had been the largest slaveholding family in Virginia in their day.

Will had been in contact for many years with some descendants of these slaves. He had recently connected with Susan Hutchinson, a descendant of Thomas Jefferson and Martha Jefferson. She and others of her family were talking to descendants of Thomas Jefferson and Sally Hemmings. Together, Will and Susan saw CJP's approach to peace and justice work as keys to the door of Dr. King's dining room, "where the sons and daughters of former slaves and the sons and daughters of former slaveowners will be able to sit down at the table of sister- and brotherhood."

Learning about CTTT made me think. Had my own family enslaved people? No one had ever mentioned it in my hearing. But the more I thought about it, the more plausible it seemed. I knew my father was from Virginia and that the family had lived there for quite a while. My father's racial prejudices had been apparent to me since I was a child. He spoke of "Colored" people disparagingly. When I was a little girl, I noticed that he, a doctor, had separate waiting rooms for "Whites" and "Colored people" at his office.

But there was another clue that I had been avoiding. When I moved to the Shenandoah Valley in 1994, I noticed that Kilbys were often mentioned in the local newspaper. They were activists and they were Black.

So I Googled the name "Kilby." Believe it or not, I had never done that before. Up came a website maintained by a Herbert Kilby, and it outlined the genealogy of my family. Most of the research had been done by Craig Kilby, a professional genealogist. I was able to trace back to my 4th great-grandparents,

John and Elizabeth Kilby, both born in Culpeper County, Virginia, in the early 1700s. (Culpeper was later split, and part of it became Rappahannock County.)

This was before the huge online presence of Ancestry.com and other genealogy websites, so it really was a gift to have so much information available online. Not surprisingly, the family tree included no information about slaves or possible African American branches. I decided that I needed to go to Culpeper and Rappahannock counties to find whatever original documents I could about these ancestors and their possible connection to slavery.

I had some time over the Christmas holidays and found a day that the Rappahannock County Historical Society was open. Located in Washington, Virginia, it was only about an hour's drive from my home. Passing over the Blue Ridge and into rural Rappahannock County was like going back in time. To this day, there is not one fast-food restaurant or chain store in this county. All you see are farm fields, woodlands, old houses, and quaint little towns and crossroads communities. Back in the 1960s, rich folks from Washington, D.C., had bought up the large historic mansions and purchased most of the farms. They made sure they instituted strict development controls to keep the land rural, beautiful, and exclusively theirs.

The residents of Washington, Virginia, fondly known as "Little Washington," brag that it is the first town in what is now the United States to be named "Washington." George Washington had made a survey of the town in July 1749. With a population of 135, it is probably best known for the Inn at Little Washington, a five-star restaurant, inn, and member of the Relais & Chateaux hotel group, which attracts "a discerning clientele from Washington, D.C., and its suburbs." It is an expensive place to dine. Lucky for me, I could find a $5 sandwich at The Country Café across the street.

As I entered the tiny brick historical society building, I was greeted by a friendly Judy Tole, Executive Director, who immediately jumped in to help me with my research. She suggested that I look first at the U.S. Census, which she had printed out in notebooks. The county population has always been so small that one Census year could be fit in a notebook. I decided to look at the 1840 Census first, a year I thought might be a high time for slavery. In 1840, the total county population including slaves was 9,257. (The U.S. Census Bureau estimates it was 7,252 on July 1, 2018.) It was easy to find my great-great-grandfather Leroy Kilby. Along with his wife, Sarah, and mother, Frances, there were nine children listed, including my great-grandfather Andrew Jackson Kilby. There were also two slaves. No names were given these slaves, just their age and gender: a female, age 35-55, and a male, age 10-24. So, there it was, handwritten in black and white. My family had enslaved people.

I found that Leroy had enslaved four people in 1830, a female and three males. It appeared that he had sold or rented out the female's husband (?) and one son (?) by 1840. What were their names? What happened to the husband and son? What were their stories?

The Historical Society had several files on the Kilbys, including notes on Leroy Kilby's will. There was no mention of slaves. Judy suggested that I go to the courthouse next door to look at the will books, records of court cases, and other legal documents to see if I could find names of slaves. They were considered property, so that is why their names might show up in county records. But before I left, Judy directed me to the books she had for sale. Among them, was *Wit, Will &*

Walls, by Betty Kilby Fisher, published in 2002. I immediately saw that Betty was African American from the photo on the cover. Also, there was another Kilby book, *I Stretch my Hands to Thee, the Kilby Legacy*, by Patricia Kilby Robb and James Wilson Kilby. Of course I bought both books, and then headed for the courthouse.

I searched and searched the will books but could not find a will for my great-great-grandfather Leroy Kilby or his brother Thomas Kilby, or any other Kilbys from the period of enslaving. So I switched to Chancery Court records and immediately struck gold—if you consider it gold to find records showing names of enslaved persons in your family records.

There was a court case filed in 1865 in which Mortimer Kilby sued his mother Malinda (Kilby) Thornhill. Malinda was Thomas Kilby's wife before she remarried. Mortimer was Thomas and Malinda's son. An excerpt of this court record provides interesting details:

"In the court of Rappahannock County in Chancery,

"Your complainant Mortimer Kilby respectfully represents that _____ [left blank] Kilby departed this life sometime since in the county of Culpeper intestate possessed of a small amount of personal estate and a servant woman named Juliet. Whatever there was of his personal property has been long disposed of and applied according to law.

"His widow Melinda Kilby now Melinda Thornhill has had possession of said slave Juliet who has given birth to several children to wit, Simon, John, James and Sarah. These slaves have been raised by said Melinda until the eldest has got to be a boy that could render some service. They are all valuable.

"Some few years since the said Melinda married Bluford Thornhill of Rappahannock County and it has become a matter of some importance that said slaves should be divided

between those entitled thereto according to their unspo-
ken rights giving to the said Melinda Thornhill her shares
therein...."

(Note: In the historical records I found, sometimes names
are spelled slightly differently. I found both "Juliet" and "Juliett," "Melinda" and "Malinda." The preponderance of the
records spells their names "Juliet" and "Malinda," so I will
refer to them as such unless quoting directly from a historical
document.)

Mortimer goes on to name himself and his brothers and
sisters as rightful heirs to these slaves, along with his mother,
and asks that the slaves be divided among these persons. The
case was never resolved because the end of the Civil War made
it moot. Juliet and her children were freed. Or were they? How
soon did they find out that they could no longer be owned as
slaves? And where would Juliet go, once free, a woman alone
with four young children?

Well, it was getting late and the courthouse was closing. I
would have to come back for the answers.

I decided to return on another day to the U.S. Census to see
what happened to Juliet and her children. The 1870 Census is
a key Census year for finding information about former slaves
because it was the first year that they were recorded as persons
with names.

I was excited as I opened the notebook in the Rappahannock Historical Society. I looked and looked, but found no sign
of Juliet or her children. They were not listed as a family, and
they were not shown as living in the household of Malinda
Kilby and her second husband Bluford Thornhill. Where did
they go? Did they leave the county? How would I find them?

So back to the courthouse I went to see what I could find
there. I looked in the marriage books and found that a Simon

Kilby married Lucy Frances Wallace in 1873. One line in the marriage book showed "Juliet" as Simon's mother, with the space for his father left blank. Wow, I thought. So, Simon was still here in Rappahannock County, despite not showing up in the Census.

The County Clerk showed me the files where the marriage licenses were kept, and I found one for Simon and Lucy Frances! Marriage licenses usually show the parents of the bride and groom, but that section on this one was blank. Attached to the license was a note written by a P.M. Finks, attesting to the

Note accompanying marriage license of Simon Kilby and Lucy Frances Wallace, 1873.

fact that Simon was of age to get married. Regarding Simon's parents, it just said that they were both dead. So maybe Juliet had died young, before 1870.

I was beginning to fill in the family tree, but there were a lot of missing branches. I spent the rest of the day in futile searches through court records and Census books. Before I left the Historical Society that day, I saw a map on the wall showing the old roads of Rappahannock County with houses and other important buildings and places located and named. This looked like a promising source of information, so I purchased a copy.

Now it was time for me to read that book, *Wit, Will & Walls*, by Betty Kilby Fisher. From the very first chapter, I began seeing clues that her family and mine might be connected. The biggest clue—her father grew up in Peola Mills, Virginia. This is an unincorporated area in Rappahannock County, near where my father grew up. I remembered this because my mother thought the name was funny and teased

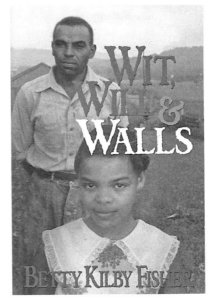

him about being from there. You would hardly know that Peola Mills is a place. It really is just a small village with a few houses. Betty's father, James Wilson Kilby, grew up on the Finks Farm. I pulled out that historical map I had bought, and there was my father's family farm, Belle Meade, directly adjacent to Dick Finks' Hill. My father must have known James Wilson Kilby, but he never said a word to me about him.

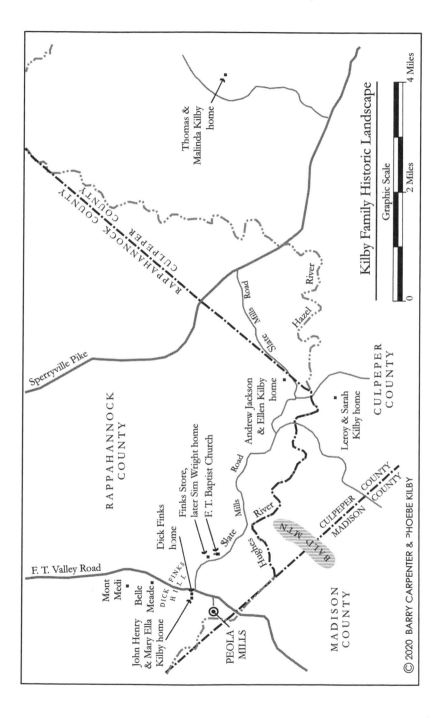

Kilby Family Historic Landscape

Graphic Scale

0   2 Miles   4 Miles

Thomas & Malinda Kilby home

RAPPAHANNOCK COUNTY

CULPEPER COUNTY

Spertryville Pike

State Mills Road

Hazel River

Andrew Jackson & Ellen Kilby home

Leroy & Sarah Kilby home

CULPEPER COUNTY

Finks Store, later Sim Wright home

F. T. Baptist Church

Dick Finks home

State Mills Road

F. T. Valley Road

Mont Medi

Belle Meade

DICK FINKS HILL

John Henry & Mary Ella Kilby home

PEOLA MILLS

Hughes River

BALD MTN

CULPEPER COUNTY

MADISON COUNTY

MADISON COUNTY

© 2020 BARRY CARPENTER & PHOEBE KILBY

Betty writes about the "pain and agony" her father and grandparents experienced working as sharecroppers for the Finks. "In moments of weakness and despair, Daddy talked about his being Black and compared his Blackness to evil, as the destructive black birds and the black cat. However, soon after he spoke the ugly words of his Blackness, he would compose himself and talk about how our African ancestors were Kings and Queens, and how they were snatched from their homeland, and boarded on ships like animals.

"He would say, 'Evil, evil, I'll tell you what's evil—robbing a man of his dignity is evil, violating my momma and sister is evil, killing my momma is evil, old man Dick Finks is evil, I am not evil with my Black skin, I am born to be great because God created me Black.'"

My eyes filled with tears as I read this. Pain just dripped off the pages. Betty and her father knew well that their family had been enslaved and that the control and oppression that continued afterwards were directly linked. You can read about Jim Crow and how sharecropping was just another form of slavery. But these words made it real. This was more than oppression; it was terrorism. I am sure my family knew about all of this and condoned it. Okay, I really do not know if they condoned these actions and attitudes, but I vividly remember my father calling Black people "coons," making clear he thought they were lesser.

I also remember my grandmother, who still lived on that farm near Peola Mills, coming to visit us one time in Baltimore when I was growing up. The maid we employed, Inez, came to the front door for work, dressed nicely as she always did, before heading to the basement to put on her uniform. My grandmother berated my mother, "How can you let that *Negro* woman come to the front door, and with those white gloves on? She should be coming to the back door and in her uniform!" To my mother's credit, she never did ask Inez to come to the back door in her uniform.

As I read on, I saw more connections, some more pleasant. Betty describes Sunday dinners of "country ham, fried chicken, string beans with ham hocks, macaroni and cheese, corn pudding, lemon meringue pie, pound cake, yeast rolls and corn bread." Those were foods we ate at my grandmother's when we visited. Betty also talks of her family making apple butter, as did mine.

Then I reached a section of her book, where she recounts how her father was cheated out of land he owned. "Old Man Dick Finks" had hired a lawyer whose name was quite familiar to me—James W. Fletcher. That was "Jim Bill Fletcher!" I really did not know any details about this man. All I knew was that my father talked about him a lot as we drove down the road to my grandmother's house. He was a cheat and not to be trusted, according to my father. It fit that Old Man Dick Finks would hire him.

This was all a preamble to reading the most amazing part of Betty's book, where she describes her struggles to get a high school education. I was truly impressed with her courage and the courage of her family. And I was appalled and saddened by her story of being raped in school. But I felt more than that. I was angry too, because I saw that her very being had been violated.

As I read her story, I had to contrast it with my own life. I had no obstacles when pursuing an education. My parents sent me to a private girls' school, where I was afforded excellent instruction in language, literature, research, and writing. My parents sent me to Duke University debt-free. Then I was awarded a full scholarship to graduate school. There could

Incomplete Family Trees for Persons Enslaved by Kilbys
(As of January 2007)

Simon Kilby

Lucy F. Wallace

John Kilby

Juliet Ann (_____)

James Kilby

Sarah Kilby

Child (Male)

Adult (Male)

Adult (Female)

Child (Male)

Enslaved by Thomas & Malinda Kilby

Enslaved by Leroy & Sarah Kilby

John Henry Kilby

Mary Ella Kilby

James Wilson Kilby

Catherine Ausberry

James M. Kilby

John F. Kilby

Betty Ann Kilby

Patricia Kilby

Gene M. Kilby

1700   1800   1900   2000

Phoebe Kilby's Family Tree (Simplified*)

* Additional information www.acommongrace.org/genealogy

1700　　　　1800　　　　1900　　　　2000

John Kilby

James Kilby

Elizabeth

Lucy Sparks

Leroy Kilby

Sarah Lee Hill

Thomas Kilby

Malinda Hawkins

Andrew Jackson Kilby

Ellen Marie Hitt

Joseph Mortimer Kilby

Martha Hume

Walter Bluford Kilby

Margaret Yowell

Phoebe Kilby

Walter Leroy Kilby

Janet Sollenberger

Margaret Kilby

not be much more difference in the educational opportunities offered a great-granddaughter of enslavers and one of enslaved persons.

I also read Betty's father's book. His sense of betrayal by his father, who helped Dick Finks cheat him of his land, is palpable. His determination to provide his kids a better education than he was allowed comes through clearly. He was taken out of school after the third grade to work on the farm. My father left Belle Meade and achieved degrees through medical school.

With all this information I collected over the Christmas holidays, I was increasingly sure that Betty and I were connected through slavery. But I did not have proof. I did not know whether Betty was related to Juliet or Simon or any other of Juliet's children. I went back to Will Hairston, the founder of Coming to the Table, who had first counseled me. I showed him my evidence and asked him for advice about what I should do next. I thought he might give me genealogical research advice.

But instead he said, "You know Phoebe, the only way you are going to find out is to contact Betty. Next week is Martin Luther King Day. That would be a good day to do it." I was not expecting that. I had to admit that this might be a necessary step, but now? I was just coming to grips with the fact that my family had enslaved people. Would Betty really want to be contacted by someone like me?

HELLO, COUSIN!

BETTY AND PHOEBE

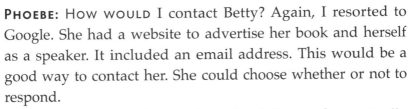

PHOEBE: HOW WOULD I contact Betty? Again, I resorted to Google. She had a website to advertise her book and herself as a speaker. It included an email address. This would be a good way to contact her. She could choose whether or not to respond.

Well, planning what to do is far different than actually doing it. I would write a few words, and then delete them. I'd try again, but no, they weren't right. I felt like I was standing on that zipline platform, putting my foot out and then pulling it back. What if I said something that upset her, or worse, insulted her? What if she responded with an email telling me off, telling me to go to hell? I tried sleeping on it.

The next day, I tried to be more thoughtful than emotional. What would a peacebuilder do? Then I thought of my classmates from the Middle East. If they could talk to each other, then I could certainly send Betty an email.

It was Martin Luther King Day 2007. I had to step off that platform now.

-----Original Message-----
From: Phoebe Kilby
Sent: Monday, January 15, 2007 9:46 AM
To: Betty Kilby Fisher
Subject: An Invitation to Conversation

Dear Betty Kilby Fisher,

My name is Phoebe Kilby, and I am white. My father grew up in Rappahannock County, VA, near where your father grew up. I have been doing some research on my family and have also read your book. Having no definitive answers, I suspect that our families had some kind of relationship in the past.

I admire very much your courage and the courage of your father and family during the Civil Rights era and since. It would be an honor to talk to you and meet you some day. I live about 25 miles from Front Royal. Through conversations, we both might find out a little more about our families' pasts.

Martin Luther King had "a dream that... the sons of former slaves and slave owners will be able to sit down together at the table of Brotherhood." Perhaps, we as daughters can contribute to fulfilling that dream.

I hope to hear from you and to hear that you are interested in conversing with me.

Phoebe Kilby

A day went by… no response. Then two, then a week, then almost two weeks. I thought, she does not want to talk to me. Why would she? I went back to Will to report the lack of response. He suggested that I talk to Prinny Anderson, another Coming to the Table participant who had more recently connected with her African American cousins, descendants of Thomas Jefferson and Sally Hemmings. I sent Prinny an email, and she suggested I try again with a longer message telling more about myself. This time I decided to bare all.…

-----Original Message-----
From: Phoebe Kilby
Sent: Monday, January 29, 2007 9:48 AM
To: Betty Kilby Fisher
Subject: Contact w/ Another Kilby?

Dear Betty Kilby Fisher,

About two weeks ago I sent the e-mail below, hoping that you would respond and that I could correspond with you. Thinking about it, I can see that you might be reluctant to contact this stranger from out of the blue. So I thought that I would tell you more about myself and my motivations for contacting you.

I am Phoebe Kilby, the daughter of Walter and Janet Kilby. I am 54 years old and grew up in Baltimore, Maryland. I now live in Shenandoah County, between Strasburg and Woodstock, so I am not very far from Front Royal, where I know you grew up. As I mentioned in my first e-mail, I have read your book.

When I was young, we used to visit my grandmother and my father's family in Rappahannock County on a farm called Belle Meade. I only have vague memories of these visits, since they stopped after my grandmother died when I was a teenager. We only visited for the day, and so I never spent much time in Rappahannock County. I was much closer to my mother's family, who lived in Woodstock.

I went to college in North Carolina, and then lived in the Washington, DC area for about 16 years. My husband and I moved to Shenandoah County in 1994. We started to read the *Northern Virginia Daily*, and that's when I became aware that there were black Kilbys. I wondered whether we were somehow related. My father died in 1986, so I could not ask him. My mother said that when she married my father, he told her that his family was not related to the Kilbys in Front Royal.

I have long had the feeling that my father had not been truthful or that perhaps his parents had told him that we had no relationship to the black Kilbys because they wanted to hide it. But I did nothing to try to find out more about our families until recently.

What prompted me to do so is related to my taking a job at Eastern Mennonite University last August. I do fundraising for the university's Center for Justice and Peacebuilding. This center has a program called "Coming to the Table," which promotes dialogue between persons whose ancestors were slave holders and persons whose ancestors were enslaved. You can

read about the program at: http://www.emu.edu/cjp/
comingtothetable/. This web site does a much better
job than I ever could to explain why these people are
talking to each other.

After talking to a participant in Coming to the Table,
I decided to go to Rappahannock County to see if
I could find out whether my ancestors had owned
slaves. I already had found a family genealogy on the
web at: http://homepages.rootsweb.com/~schulthe/
Genes/Kilby/reports/JohnKilbyNGS.htm. By tracing
from my father back, I was able to determine that my
great great grandfather, Leroy Kilby, lived during the
early 1800s. I checked his will (1859), and there was no
mention of slaves. I also checked Census data. While
the 1850 census did not provide information on slaves,
the 1840 Census did. It showed that Leroy Kilby
owned 2 slaves, a male (age between 10 and 24) and
a female (age between 36 and 55). Could your family
be descendants of these slaves? I am not sure. Leroy
Kilby had a brother Thomas, who also had slaves: a
woman, Juliet, and her four children: Simon, John,
James, and Sarah. Leroy's and Thomas's grandfather,
John, had one slave at his death as noted in his will. So
the white Kilbys of Rappahannock County were slave
holders.

Perhaps the most telling information I collected at
the Rappahannock County Historical Society was a
map prepared in 1999 showing the names of historic
family homes in Rappahannock County. Right next to
my father's family farm, Belle Meade, was Dick Fink's

Hill! Leroy Kilby's farm is a mile or two to the south. The fact that your father grew up on the farm next door to my father's family farm seems very significant to me. Perhaps if we dig deeper, we could find more about our families' connections.

I read your father's book and noted in it what appeared to me to be his longing for more information about his roots. Perhaps you and your brothers and sister have the same longing. I would like to share my research with you, and perhaps we can piece this together.

As I said in the following e-mail, I admire very much the courage of your family during the Civil Rights era. At the same time, I feel shame that my family once owned slaves and obviously by that very fact traumatized and mistreated them. Someone in the Kilby family needs to apologize for this injustice and perhaps that person should be me.

I have provided my e-mail address and phone numbers in the following e-mail. I hope that you will contact me.

Phoebe Kilby

Within a few hours, I heard back from Betty. She called me first, but I was on the phone. So she left me a message. She was very emotional, very glad that I had contacted her. She told me that her book had been made into a short film and that two screenings were planned in February. She would be in Front Royal in February, and she wanted me to meet her family and come to the screenings. Her email came soon after the phone message:

-----Original Message-----
From: Betty Kilby Fisher
Sent: Monday, January 29, 2007 12:26 PM
To: Phoebe Kilby
Subject: Hello Cousin

Phoebe,

If you are asking yourself why I am so emotional, the cultural-innovations email address gets full of spam mail and is often down. I went to that site this morning and emails began to download. It could have only been God.

We are the key to healing. Meeting you today is so awesome. People will find it hard to believe, I can't believe! I have always known the we were descendants of slaves but I couldn't open that door.

I want you to come to all three of these events. I want you to introduce yourself and talk about our connection. Bring your camera crews from "Coming to the Table." We can not only contribute to Dr. King's dream. We can bring about racial reconciliation and healing to a nation of hurting people.

I thank God for bringing you into my life.

Betty Kilby Fisher

"Hello Cousin" as the subject line—I was truly touched. And her email was so open and welcoming. I did not know if we were cousins, but I felt honored that she had opened her heart enough to call me "Cousin."

"Truth and Mercy have met together..."

BETTY: I was focused on selling my book during those months, boarding a plane practically every Thursday, each time going to a place I had never been, a place where I didn't know a single soul, renting a vehicle that I most likely was not familiar with, and driving to my destination with only MapQuest directions.

I slept in spaces available through Military Lodging on military bases all over these United States. That means as I traveled to these bases, I didn't have a confirmed reservation, and I wasn't sure if I would have to go off base to find lodging at night when I finished selling books at the military store (PX: BX: NEX). My husband at the time was military retired, and I had my military ID. He had a pretty high classification, and most of the time I did get to stay in Military Lodging.

I was a single grandmother of two school-age children. I had no job and was separated from my husband. If I didn't sell books, I couldn't feed these grandchildren. I was expected to be back home by the time they served donuts at the church on Sunday morning; otherwise the babysitter would have two upset children to comfort. They had a fear of my not being there for them.

From the time I arrived at a military base, it was all about selling books. I had a 30-second elevator speech, and I spoke to everyone that came within speaking range. My sales exceeded the Business Service Manager's expectation. I worked from the time I arrived at the base exchange until it closed. I was back at my signing booth the first thing on Friday and Saturday mornings at the opening of the exchange until the store closed.

Most of the time I packed my lunch from the breakfast buffet at base lodging and only took necessity breaks. I had Monday through Wednesday to plan my trips and get my two grandchildren ready for my next Thursday trip. To say I was busy was an understatement.

Phoebe confirmed what I suspected all the time, that I was spiritually connected to my ancestors. There was a Betty Ann Kilby in the White school in Rappahannock County who made the honor roll. I cut the article out of the newspaper and pretended it was me. I had hoped to someday find the White Kilbys, and here she was. Phoebe did what I couldn't, and she was willing to share her research. God knows that I didn't have time to do the research. She admired the courage of my family, which reassured me.

One time I did a presentation, "Why My Daddy Did What He Did," at the Historical Society in Front Royal. After the presentation, we called for questions, and this White woman stood up and said, "We hated your father." There was a pause and I said, "Lord, have mercy," quietly to myself. She went on to say, "He disrupted everybody's life, but we knew that it was necessary for y'all to get an education. He was a great and brave man."

I never got her out of my head. She was not the only White person who felt that way. At that point in my life, I wanted to bring about racial reconciliation and healing to my community. I had no idea how to accomplish it. I had my hands full raising my grandchildren. God never worked on my schedule, but he heard my prayer and he sent Phoebe to help.

Phoebe had me when she quoted Dr. King to me. This White woman suggesting that we could live Dr. King's dream? What a fantastic way to honor Dr. King. It was only natural for me to invite her to the family dinner and to the premiere of the documentary.

DINNER AND A MOVIE

BETTY AND PHOEBE

7

BETTY: IN 2005, I was in Germany selling and signing my book. One day as I was checking my emails, up pops one from Paulette Moore. I had done a TV interview with her in 2004 for the 50th anniversary of the Brown vs. Board of Education decision, and I remembered her name. She asked me if I was interested in doing a short documentary on my story.

I'm glad I was in the privacy of my room because I did my happy dance. I started to email her back. I was partially in disbelief that this was happening, but maybe it was a hoax. I had made several contacts inquiring about a potential documentary when I first started selling my book. I was rejected, or informed of the cost, or I didn't receive any response at all. Now I was at a loss for words. I responded only with, "Yes."

The next evening when I checked my emails, Paulette had laid out a plan. I explained that I was in Germany but that I would contact her when I got home. By the time I returned, Paulette was already at work on a grant. She would contact me and say, "I need you to come." I would say, "Yes," before she could say when and where.

Once she asked me to come to Winchester, Virginia, to meet with a youth group. I was to tell them my story while they painted from their imaginations about what I was telling them. The youth group's paintings were used as a backdrop for the documentary. This adventure was so exciting for me. Paulette kept me in the loop with every phase of the project.

She was hiring actors, including someone to play me. After she had interviewed several professionals and wasn't satisfied, I suggested that she interview my granddaughter, Tanesia. Tanesia had read the book several times. Every time she got in trouble in school, my son Tony would make her write a report on various aspects of the book. Paulette interviewed her and hired her to play me. She hired a professional to play my dad. I was present for all the filming. The whole experience was a great boost to my confidence. I began to feel that I was important.

Tanesia Fisher, Betty's granddaughter, portraying Betty in the film, *Wit, Will & Walls.*

Daddy always said, "We should have a movie. After all, it was our case that brought about the first desegregation in Virginia." I was beginning to think he was right. He believed that if we could get the information to Oprah, our story would make it to the big screen.

In 2000, I tried to get to Oprah. I kept calling in to get tickets to her show. I would call, get the busy signal, hang up, call again. This went on all day. One evening, very late, I got through and was put on hold. After holding several hours, I was informed that the line was closed and that I should try again tomorrow. I was so disappointed.

I was glad that I didn't tell Daddy what I was trying to do. Our documentary was not the movie he imagined, but it was pretty close. He died in 2003, but I bet he would have been real proud of me for living Dr. King's dream and for the 16-minute documentary that was underway.

I rarely thought about a trip until it was the next event on the schedule. As February 17, 2007, approached, I realized it was 48 years and one day since Jimmy, John, and I had walked up the hill to integrate Warren County High School. I had come a long way since that historic day. I couldn't help but believe that it was my day and my time.

But my family thought that all the changes in my life in a short period of time were affecting my mental capacity. They insisted that I call everybody who was invited to the celebration dinner and the premiere showing of the documentary and tell them that *White* Kilbys were coming, too. Calling my family made me wonder if I had made an insane move. Not everyone agreed to come to the dinner. But the ones who came were the ones who were supposed to be there.

The experience caused me to have a little talk with my ancestors. My grandmother Kilby died the year that I was born, so I never met her. But her spirit was with me all the days of my life. Late in one midnight hour, I called on her spirit. She said she endured all that life threw at her down here on earth, but now she was in the land of "no mo work, no mo sickness, no mo heartache, no mo pain, and no mo sorrow, and it was the right thing to heal the hurting world the best I could." With these thoughts, I moved forward.

I felt good at the meal. Phoebe was a brave soul to come to dinner at a table where she was surrounded by African Americans. She had the good sense to bring her sister along. If she was willing to take such a risk, she had my respect and my friendship. It felt great to introduce Phoebe and her sister as my cousins. I have a mischievous nature, and I enjoyed the shock factor. I watched for people's reaction to the news. With all that we do to honor Dr. King's birthday and honor Black History Month, I didn't know anyone at that point who could say they were living his dream.

PHOEBE: I was more excited about meeting Betty and her family than fearful about how they might react to me. But I decided to ask my sister Margaret to go with me so I wouldn't be all by myself. I checked with Betty first, and she was okay with Margaret coming.

February 17, the evening of the dinner, was cold. Snow threatened. Betty had asked us to come to her mother's house in Front Royal before the dinner, which would be followed by the film screening at the Old Schoolhouse Theater in the tiny village of Reliance, only a few miles from Front Royal. I had been to the theater previously to see a play by a Shenandoah University theater group, so I knew where it was.

When Margaret and I arrived at Catherine Kilby's (Betty's mother's) house, I knocked on the side door off the carport. An older woman with a cane met us at the door. I introduced myself, but she did not know who I was or why I was there. I said that we came to meet Betty, so she invited us in. We sat at the kitchen table and were beginning to visit when the phone rang.

Mrs. Kilby was across the kitchen table from the phone and was having trouble getting up, so Margaret picked up the phone. It was Betty. She had tried to reach me on my cell phone, which I had turned off. (I'm bad about that.) There was a change in plans. We were to meet her and the rest of the family at the Main Street Mill Restaurant in downtown Front Royal.

Margaret and I had brought a cake for the family, so we left it with Catherine Kilby, thanked her for her hospitality, and left to join Betty. I was amazed by Mrs. Kilby's willingness to let us into her house. Two White women whom she didn't know had knocked on her door, and she had welcomed us into her kitchen. The apple does not fall far from the tree.

When Margaret and I entered the restaurant, we saw a Black family at a table. Two young women introduced themselves, Bettina and Renee, Betty's daughters. They were very

Betty's daughters Bettina Fisher and Renee Gibbs.

friendly and approachable. Their mother was in the restroom. When Betty came into the dining room, she came over to give me a big hug. We both exclaimed how happy we were to meet and sat down to order dinner.

As we ate, Margaret and I learned that Bettina and Renee both lived in the D.C. area. At the time, Bettina was a project manager working on special projects and events for American University. Renee was property manager for a commercial real estate management company. One of the properties that she managed was the Warner Theater. Margaret lived near American University, and we both had attended shows at the Warner Theater. We could have walked right past Bettina or Renee sometime in the past and not known that they were our cousins.

BETTY: Bettina and Renee grew up in integrated schools. They had White friends. They themselves were successful and aspiring young African American women. They encouraged me in everything that I was doing, and they supported me in my endeavors. My brother John wanted to know where was his 40 acres and a mule? You could clearly see the different attitudes of the various generations.

Not every member of my family agreed with everything that I was doing. It didn't really matter to me what they thought. I had proven them wrong with every stumbling block they threw at me. They said I wouldn't succeed in school. I had my Associate's degree, my Bachelor's degree and my Master's degree. They said I wouldn't hold down a job for more than a couple of months. In 1986, I broke through the concrete ceiling to become the highest ranking African American female at a Fortune 500 company. They said that I would be lucky if I sold 50 books; I had already sold almost 25,000.

I think every time I was told that something couldn't be done, I worked hard to make it happen. I told myself, "I will not fail, and I will not quit." Yes, there were times that I failed, but it wasn't because I didn't give it my all, and they became successes turned inside out. On this night, I was going to enjoy every facet of the new journey.

PHOEBE: After a while, Betty's brother, James, came in and sat in the empty chair next to me. While Betty was very open to me, James was more circumspect. I told him a little about myself and Coming to the Table. He muttered something to the effect that he had seen White people come to the table before, but they usually did not stick around. Finally, he said, "I just have to ask you, what are your politics?" I told him that I was a lifelong Democrat and that I did not support George Bush. Somehow Ronald Reagan came up, and I said that he was the beginning of our country's Republican revolution and its favoring of the haves over the have-nots and Whites over persons of color. James started to warm up to me a little.

While I was talking to James, Betty's daughters paid for dinner. I had planned to pay, but they had already done it! Now it was time to head to the theater. It was snowing pretty hard, and the Kilbys were not familiar with the location of the theater. I offered to lead them, since I had been there before. All the way to the theater, I worried that I might make a mistake and go the wrong way. I had come to the theater before from I-81. This time I was taking them from Front Royal via Route 340-522. But we got there without any trouble. I recognized the white church across the street where we could park.

The theater was already filling up, even on this very snowy night. Will Hairston, Amy Potter, and Jan Jenner from EMU had come to the show all the way from Harrisonburg. I introduced them to the Kilbys. I had brought my camera, so we had people take pictures of Margaret and me with Betty and James. I found out that James had his own book, *The Forever Fight*, and bought a copy from him, which he autographed. He signed it, "To: Phoebe and Margaret, Peace and Love, James M. Kilby, 2-17-07." I treasure this.

Paulette Moore, the filmmaker from Shenandoah University, introduced her 16-minute film of Betty's struggle to get a high school education at Warren County High School—"Wit, Will & Walls, the Betty Kilby Fisher Story." The film was very well done, and I was caught up in the story and impressed by Betty's bravery as a young girl and as a woman. After this first film, Paulette introduced a second film—4 minutes long—by her students, who interviewed Tanesia, Betty's granddaughter, who plays Betty in the first film.

Betty followed with a presentation about her experiences and how hard it had been for her to write her book on which the film was made. She had had an easy time with chapters 1 and 2, but when it came to chapter 3, she froze. It was too painful. She had to go into her closet to write.

BETTY: Many times when giving a presentation, I would not interact with the audience beforehand. I still had triggers and flashbacks that could make me cry. Besides, this was also Tanesia's night. I wanted to introduce my son, Tony, his wife Lyn, my grandson, Tyler, and, of course, Tanesia, to as many people as possible.

Tony usually picked me up at the airport and got me to the taping locations. Quite often the taping took place in the middle of book signings, so Tony had to take me back to the airport for my next assignment. I wanted him to know that I appreciated him, and what I was doing was passing our story on to the next generation.

Tanesia was comfortable hanging out with the students from Shenandoah University who directed the short film. They were laughing about filming at my mother's house when they had to stop and cut because my mother was making noise. When they explained why they needed silence, she said, "This is my house. I will do as I please." Mom didn't understand the filming process. They were respectful and waited for her to finish her chips. But Mom continued to interrupt until it became funny and impossible to continue the filming. They ended up remaking the film at Tanesia's house in Lansdowne, Virginia, and at her school, Stonebridge High School.

PHOEBE: At the end of her presentation, Betty surprised everyone by introducing me and Margaret to the audience as her cousins. She told them we were descended from slaveholders who had held her ancestors, and that I had recently contacted her. I had not prepared to speak, but I decided that I should. I told the audience that I had met Betty for the first time just a few hours earlier, and that she and her family could not have been more gracious. I told them that I was honored to meet her and was looking forward to getting to know her more and to sharing our stories.

I said goodbye to the Kilbys and took Margaret back to her car. I wasn't sure that I would attend the second film screening the next afternoon. The dinner and this event had been so meaningful and wonderful, I wasn't sure that the next day could be nearly as good. It could be a letdown.

When I got up the next morning, a Sunday, I decided that I really wanted to go to the next screening at Mt. Carmel Baptist Church in Winchester. I did a digital search for the location and saw that it was next to Shenandoah University on Pleasant Valley Road. I drove in the snow, and somehow drove by the church without seeing it. The map didn't indicate which side of the street the church was on. I was worried that I would be late and that that would be disrespectful. But I entered the church just in time, and a woman directed me into the sanctuary. I could see immediately that I was under-dressed. Everyone else was still in their Sunday finest at 4:00 in the afternoon. The sanctuary had a good crowd in it, with many more Black people than the night before.

There was a band on the stage and some excellent singers. The place was rocking. Betty was on stage clapping and singing, and the audience joined in.

After the music, Paulette spoke a bit about the films and showed them. Then she introduced Betty, who gave a similar presentation to the one the evening before. At the end, she again introduced me as her cousin, the descendant of the slaveholders that had held her ancestors. She said, "I want you to know that she contacted me, and in her email, she included Martin Luther King, Jr.'s line, the one where he had a dream that 'the sons of former slaves and slave owners will be able to sit down together at the table of brotherhood.'"

The crowd erupted in applause, and people came up to shake my hand. It was a very moving experience. I really felt that somehow, I represented for that brief instant the kind of White person these Black people were hoping for—someone to apologize for what happened to Betty and for the legacy of slavery. This was probably wishful thinking on my part, but people seemed to be genuinely glad that I was there. I just wanted to be sure not to draw too much attention to myself. This was Betty's moment.

The minister came to shake my hand and insisted that I have my photo taken with him and Betty. I asked Betty's nephew to take a picture of Betty, James, and me.

This was a wonderful moment, as you can see.

BETTY: I had succeeded one more time with the help of so many diverse people, and now I had another challenge. Phoebe invited me to a Coming to the Table event in Memphis. I dreamed as did Dr. King of a society founded on justice, equality, and love for all. Together, we found that. We were about to embark upon a challenge to change the world, one cousin at a time.

Betty Kilby Fisher (Baldwin), Phoebe Kilby, James M. Kilby, February 18, 2007.

LOVE, WAR, AND PEACE

BETTY

1989 TO '91 was a time of reckoning for me and realizing what love has to do with life. Why was I always at war personally, and how could I find peace?

I started to work for Rubbermaid on January 15, 1979, and I retired from Rubbermaid on January 15, 1989. I purposely started and ended my employment on Martin Luther King's birthday. Many places of business did not close for the MLK National Holiday. However, it was a paid holiday at Rubbermaid. I started as a Level 3 Customer Service Representative, and I ended as a Level 18 Scheduler. By 1986 I had become the highest ranking African American female at Rubbermaid.

I started there with a high school education. Through the company's tuition reimbursement program, I was leaving with a supervision certificate, an Associate's degree and a Bachelor's degree, and I was two classes from having earned my MBA. But I left broken-hearted because I had to fight for every promotion and every accomplishment. No matter how much I accomplished, I was still second-class in the workplace. Twenty-five years after I fought for an education, I still had to fight and depend on the law to get what was rightfully mine in the workplace.

My mother had a stroke. I realized that if she had died, I would have been in torment the rest of my life because I had not forgiven her for what I perceived as her not protecting me during those years of desegregation.

Women in those days had no voice. They were taught to submit to their husbands, and Momma was a dutiful wife. She only confronted Daddy in the privacy of their bedroom. While I had stepped outside the traditional role of wife, I realized that my mother continued to be the wife she was brought up to be.

When I interviewed Daddy for a school paper, he told me how one day at work someone threw a hammer at him. He said he could hear it whistle as it passed his head. He said he went into a stairwell, and he could not get the words out to pray, so he prayed in his heart.

He told me how on another occasion there was no "out of order" sign on the elevator, so he punched the button and the elevator opened. With one step, he could have been killed. Even when we became adults, Daddy said not a day went by that he did not pray for us. He said he had made it a habit to always pray for us. I forgave him then, because on that day I understood him.

There was no opportunity for me to ask Momma why she did not stop Daddy during the integration movement. I had come to understand that Daddy had to make sure that we all got an education. I began to remember Momma's sacrifices. I wanted this red blazer, and Momma searched to find that red blazer on sale. When she could not find it on sale, she bought it at full price just for me. Reflecting on the things I was doing for my children helped me to clearly see the things Momma had done for me.

The first time a White man apologized to me for what his people did during desegregation, I did not know what to say. After sleeping on it, the next time someone apologized for the things that I endured, I said it was God's journey for me. Then I realized that only God had power over my situation, and Momma could not change what God set in motion. I forgave her and began to work on our relationship.

My daughter Erika announced that she was pregnant by Tommy Jones, a White boy who took her to the prom. It seemed like everything was attacking me at once. When I realized that she was getting too involved with this boy, I had sent her to work for my sister in Washington, D.C. She was miserable. She returned to Front Royal and moved in with Tommy. I had to accept that I could not choose who she should fall in love with, and that her baby with both bloods running through his veins was my grandchild to love no matter what.

I wanted to hang up my boxing gloves. I wanted peace.

The doctor said that if Momma could make it through the year after her stroke, she would live to be 90. The family all worked together, reading and doing everything that we could think of to make sure it happened.

During that time, I was working on my last two classes to complete my MBA. I spent fun time with Momma, getting to know her and loving her the way a daughter should. We went to exercise together. We went out to eat, just the two of us. That's when I learned that Momma ate dessert before the main meal. When I got after her, she said, "Y'all grown now. I don't have to be an example." So we both ate our desserts first, followed by the main meals, and then we each ordered another dessert so we could end our meals with something sweet.

I remember Momma saying as we were growing up, "Get up, put your street clothes on and your makeup, because you never know when somebody is going to come by and offer you a ride to go on an adventure." I was going to do some research at the Library of Virginia in Richmond. I dropped by the house, and, sure enough, Momma was ready. As I was driving down the road at 80 mph in my 1984 BMW, Momma would say, "You are such a good driver." Through love and relationship, we were able to mend as mother and daughter.

I took Erika to most of her doctor appointments. We would also go on long rides through the countryside. We would ride 50-60 miles just to get ice cream. We talked, laughed, and cried together. Oftentimes, it was the three of us—Erika, Momma, and me.

The day before the baby's scheduled delivery date, the doctor did a test by sticking a long needle into Erika's abdomen. When I saw the needle, I passed out. I was supposed to go in the delivery room with her, but the doctors barred me from that—which relieved me—because she was supposed to have a C-section. Instead, I smoked two cigarettes as I paced the floor, and I do not even smoke. I got the cigarettes from a man who was in the waiting room with me. He was waiting to hear the news of his wife's delivery.

On May 4, 1989, when the nurse bought that little bundle of joy into the waiting room and I held that little baby boy, my heart filled with so much love I thought it would burst wide open. I remembered what love is. I had felt that same love with the birth of every one of my 4 children.

The social worker came into Erika's room to get information for the birth certificate. She told Erika that because the child was half White, she could put White or Black on the birth certificate. The rage stirred up in me, and I asked, "Why can't he just be American?" She ignored me and again asked Erika what race, and I yelled, "American!" They kicked me out of the room, and I knew that they put "Black."

I went out and bought clothes for a boy and bedding to set up a room for him at Erika's place and a room at my house. I was trying to get accustomed to the title "Grandma." I was going to keep the baby some of the time while Erika worked. I walked back to

Betty's mother, Catherine Kilby, Betty, and Betty's grandson Eric Jones.

Erika's room, bringing a cute little boy's outfit. I learned that his name was Eric David Jones.

———◆———

I chose Dr. Martin Luther King for a paper I needed to write for one of my degree programs. I thought it would be an easy project since I had met him one time ever so briefly and because I was part of the March on Washington and heard his "I have a dream speech." I thought I knew everything. Over the years, you would have thought the only thing King did was "I have a dream." I wanted new material to write about.

I was looking at titling my paper, "Dr. King, the Man, the Mission, and the Relevance for the Workplace." So many people wanted to talk about how far African Americans had come. They seemed disappointed if I talked about how hard we had to continue to work to achieve justice. I was thinking reconciliation and the Beloved Community, but I could not see reconciliation and the Beloved Community being lived in most workplaces.

I did the research and wrote my paper about racism, justice, and equal opportunity. I was intrigued with the information I found on the Beloved Community, but that subject was more for my personal use.

It really caught my attention when Dr. King said, "The aftermath of violence is emptiness and bitterness. The aftermath of nonviolence is reconciliation and the creation of the Beloved Community."

My journey up the corporate ladder was not violent, but I sure felt empty when I left. I did not feel bitterness, because Daddy always made us pray for the people who hurt us. He said that otherwise, it was like taking poison to hurt our enemy, when all we did was hurt ourselves. I had learned that lesson. We practiced nonviolence during desegregation 25 years earlier, but it did not end with reconciliation and the Beloved Community.

Feeling all this love for my brand new grandbaby, I wanted to explore this love for all humanity that Dr. King talked about. When you start talking love, most people think only about romantic love. Dr. King referred to four kinds of love: empathy bond, friend bond, romantic love, and unconditional "God" love. Being brought up in the church, I knew God's love. Were it not for God's love, I never would have made it through the difficult times. I was familiar with most of the Scriptures pertaining to love.

I could find a connection to each of the four types of love in my everyday life. I understood love better than most. Many people in my social strata were not interested in creating the

Beloved Community. I put information about the Beloved Community on the back burner of my brain.

Love was blossoming all around me. Bettina married a nice African American man from a nice family with a similar upbringing. Her wedding colors were black and white. She finished college and landed a good job. Her husband had an apartment, a good job, and was continuing to work toward his degree. Ten months later, I was blessed with Andrew David Owens on July 31, 1990, so much love wrapped in such a small package.

My son Tony was in the Army in Germany, and he met a girl from the Philippines who was living in Germany. They were going to have a baby, too.

Tanesia Renee Fisher was born September 15, 1990. We were all excited about the love and diversity that was occurring in our family. I could not be there for her birth, but even

Four generations. Seated: Catherine Kilby, Betty's mother. Standing, from left: Eric Jones, Ashley Jones, Serenity Jones, Gabriel Byrd, Betty, Ariyanna Jones, Erika Fisher Smith.

though I wasn't able to hold her the day she was born, I could feel the love.

I was ready to go back to work. I started at mid-level management as an individual contributor with Atlantic Coast Airline. A year later, I received an offer to work at Northwest Airlink—with more money, a supervisory position, and a move to Memphis, Tennessee. I accepted the job and relocated.

I was in a bigger league now. I did not realize that when my boss wanted me to lie to the husband of a female employee, I could get fired for not following orders. No job was worth my getting in trouble with God. When I realized that there was no hope for me otherwise in that job, I endured for a year. Then I began looking for employment elsewhere. I interviewed for a management position with American Eagle the day after I was fired from Northwest Airlink. That issue did not come up, and I did not volunteer the information. I was hired and again got a raise.

This corporation had a wonderful job opportunity system. All employment opportunities were posted on a site so everyone had a chance to apply. I saw myself as an upwardly mobile African American woman. I rose from mid-level management to upper-level management in a short period of time. I was having a great experience until 9-11 hit.

The staff in my department were either lawyers or held MBAs. I qualified because of my education and experience.

The boss who hired me had retired. My new boss was a White woman who boasted that she did not get to her level through any special programs. We clashed at every corner.

I had begun to look for another opportunity because she did not hide her dislike for me. I knew that 9-11 gave her the perfect opportunity to get rid of the only African American in her department. I was not surprised when I was laid off. I had cleaned my office in anticipation of the move.

When she gave me the news I stood up, stretched forth my hand, and thanked her for the lessons learned. I thought about Daddy at my granddaddy's funeral. I had to smile because I was sure I was behaving as he had.

She said, "What, no hug?" I turned around and hugged her, knowing I was not beaten down and that I already had my next move planned. I knew I would always have to fight because I could not hide my blackness. Even the best companies sometimes hire and promote rotten managers. And it is hard to fight your boss and win.

I took my severance money, used the time off to write my story, and published it myself. I wanted the world to know that while there are companies trying to do the right thing, companies are made of individuals who can cover their tracks and get away with evil activity. I retired from working at public corporations to working for myself.

The Coronavirus pandemic brought more changes to my extended family. My brother Gene retired to move in with our mother to coordinate her care. When her money ran out, she was able to get partial care through social services, but it was not enough to provide adequate care for her at home. So Gene went back to work to bring in some more income. But then he lost his job because of the pandemic.

I was quarantined in Texas, and my sister was quarantined in Maryland with a high-risk husband, leaving my two brothers to care for Momma for the 16 hours each day not covered by social services. Gene was pushing 70, and Jimmy was in his late 70s. As Momma's condition worsened, my husband and I left Texas without reservations, not knowing where we would be able to park on the 1,316-mile journey to get to my mother. Because of the pandemic, many of the usual places where we would park overnight were closed. Flying was out of the question because of our age, medical issues, and potential difficulties if we became sick with the virus.

We made it as far as Tennessee when my brother called to say that Momma had passed in her sleep—alone—in the nursing home. It was comforting to know that God came to get her, and that she went home to be with my father who passed 17 years earlier.

On May 25, 2020, five days after my mother's death, a White police officer knelt on the neck of George Floyd, a Black man, for eight minutes and 46 seconds. I saw the emotionless look on this killer's face as he pushed the life out of another human being.

During the Civil Rights Movement, it was the image of Emmett Till in a casket with his body mutilated beyond recognition, pictured in *Jet Magazine,* that cried out to me. It was the memory of burning and looting when Dr. Martin Luther King was killed. I had not called Emmett Till's and Dr. King's deaths murder until now—as I saw George Floyd being purposely killed.

I remembered Daddy's adamant warning when the police came to our house to take Jimmy off to jail for that rock-throwing event. He told us that the police could legally kill us and get away with it. Old fears entered my spirit. Judging from what I saw with George Floyd, along with the stories and memories of other police killings, I felt that Daddy's teachings were still true.

I was stopped by the Front Royal police three years prior to Momma's death. Two police cars pulled up behind me. It was all I could do to maintain my composure. From the time I saw the red lights, I began to pray. One officer came to my window, and the other came to the passenger window. The officer at my window asked if I realized how fast I was going? I told him that I looked at my odometer when I saw his light, and I was going about 35 mph. I had stopped just past the 35-mph sign.

He informed me that the area in front of the houses on 6th Street was 25 mph. I did not argue. He gave me a ticket for going 35 mph in a 25-mph zone. I went to court. My brother Jimmy went with me. I was so nervous that I left my folder at my mother's house. Jimmy went back to get it. My case was called before Jimmy got back. The judge cut the cost of the ticket in half, but I had to pay the court costs.

I changed my driving habits and remind myself regularly of the safety rules of being African American in these United States: Never get caught alone. Be extra careful while out at night. Do not argue. Keep your hands in plain sight. Do not make any quick moves. Pray. I refuse to live in fear, but I always try to be careful.

————•————

My brother Gene called to tell me that he was speaking at the "Front Royal Unites" march. Old Man Fear was upon me, and I said, "When? Where? David and I will meet you at the house. "

Upon arriving at the Bing Crosby Stadium, I was shocked by the size and diversity of the crowd. There

From left: Gene Kilby, Betty Baldwin, David Baldwin, and James M. Kilby. Front Royal Unites event in Front Royal, VA, 2020.

were so many young people. My fear faded as I felt the love and community of the crowd.

As my mind revisited the past, my heart was filled with hope that a change was going to come. The local Coming to The Table group also gave a presentation.

I know that Phoebe and I are on the right track and that we are going to be a part of the change. Phoebe in North Carolina carries on her work to unify both races, while I work with my brothers in Virginia. We are change.

AUNT LUCIA AND COUSIN TIM

9

PHOEBE

AFTER I FIRST met Betty and her family, I wasn't sure what would happen next. Betty was back in Texas, so I would have to find creative ways to continue to connect with her. Amy Potter at CJP was applying for grants for the Coming to the Table program and beginning to set up speaking engagements at conferences to give it visibility, but no dates were yet nailed down. So I began reading books about others who had gone on a similar journey.

I found *Slaves in the Family*, by Edward Ball (2014), and *The Hairstons: An American Family in Black and White*, by Henry Weincek (2000), to be definitely worth reading if you decide to reach across the lines of division between descendants of enslavers and descendants of persons enslaved.

My husband, Barry, and I decided to visit Montpelier, former home of James Madison. We like old houses and knew that this one was being brought back to its historical configuration at the time when Madison owned it. They offered an enslaved community site tour, which provided added incentive. But the tour was disappointing. The guide did not provide much information and seemed to disparage a group of African Americans descended from Madison's slaves, who had come the weekend before for a ceremony at the slave cemetery.

I did find two useful books at the bookstore:

- *We Lived in a Little Cabin in the Yard*, edited by Belinda Hurmence (1994), and
- *Finding Oprah's Roots: Finding Yours*, by Henry Louis Gates, Jr. (2007).

The first was interesting, because it is a compendium of slave narratives from Virginia compiled by the Federal Writers' Project. None of the slaves who gave their stories were enslaved by Kilbys as far as I can tell. The second book provides helpful ideas about how to do genealogical research on African Americans.

For the next few summers, I took a week of my vacation to do more research on Betty's and my family connections. My research took me back to Rappahannock County, and also to Culpeper and Madison counties next door. The earliest records were in Culpeper; later records were in the other two counties. Madison was split off from Culpeper in 1792; Rappahannock in 1833. The families had not moved much, but the names and official records of the counties where they lived had changed.

I first visited the Culpeper County courthouse, since I could see from the online White Kilby family tree that my great-great-grandfather Leroy and his brother Thomas Kilby both died in that county. Maybe I would find more names of the persons they had enslaved.

I found Leroy Kilby's will from 1859. It simply stated that he left his land (135 acres on which he resides) and all his personal property to his wife, Sarah L. Kilby, for all her natural life. No mention of slaves.

Then I found an estate inventory for Thomas Kilby, who died in 1834. Among the many property items listed were horses, sheep, pigs, cows, several ploughs, household items, one crop of corn in the field, and…

"A Negro boy Henry

A Negro Woman Sarah & her child Juliett Ann"

Estate inventory of Thomas Kilby, brother of Phoebe's great-great-grandfather, Leroy Kilby, 1834.

Wow! Now I had Juliet's mother's name—Sarah. Where had she come from? I found records of an estate sale for Malinda Kilby's father, James Hawkins, at which Thomas purchased Sarah and Henry in 1833. So now I had records confirming Sarah's existence back to 1833. Unfortunately, I have never found any other information about Henry.

In Madison County, I learned more about Simon Kilby, Juliet's oldest son. I found him buying eight acres of land on "Ball's Mountain" in 1898. A map of Madison County showing historic roads, homes, and place names locates a "Bald Mountain" right at the intersection of the Rappahannock, Culpeper, and Madison lines, just down the road from Dick Fink's Hill.

So Simon had moved across the line to Madison County, though it seems he went to church in Rappahannock County. The minister who signed his marriage certificate was A.M. Grimsley. I had a booklet about the history of F.T. Baptist Church, located near Peola Mills, where my grandparents and father had attended. According to the booklet, Aldridge M. Grimsley became pastor in 1861 and was still there in 1873, when Simon was married.

I also found Simon (listed as Simeon) with wife "Fannie" (a nickname for Lucy Frances?) in the Madison County Census for 1900. They had a son John, 15 years old. Could that be Betty's grandfather, John Henry?

But then Simon disappears. In 1910, 1920, and 1930, I found only a Charles W. Kilby and his wife "Lucy F." Did Simon die and Lucy Frances marry Charles? I could not find a marriage certificate for them. And John does not appear in this Kilby household.

I find Betty's grandfather John in the Fink's household in Rappahannock County starting in 1920, but it looks as though this John would have been born around 1882. In 1900, he would have been 18, not 15. This was becoming confusing.

(Again, please note: One thing you learn when doing genealogical work is that records of people's and place names, as well as other data, are often slightly off. Census-takers can be sloppy when writing down names and recording ages. "Simon" is recorded as "Simeon." Lucy Frances is sometimes called "Fannie" and sometimes "Lucy F." Some people might call a mountain "Bald Mountain," and others, "Ball's Mountain." That's why it is important to obtain information from at least two sources, the more the better.)

I decided to visit my Aunt Lucia, the only Kilby of my father's generation still alive. She married into the Kilby family, but I knew she had an avid interest in the history of Rappahannock County. She was on the board of the Historical Society. At the time, Aunt Lucia lived in a very old house named Mont Medi, the log portion of which dates to 1750. It is located next to Belle Meade where my father grew up. I remember visiting her, my Uncle Billy, and my cousins Bill and Mary Moore when I was a child. Aunt Lucia used to have to cook in the "summer kitchen," which is a separate building from the house. In the 1700s and 1800s in rural Virginia, kitchens were often built separate from the house. That way the house could be saved if a kitchen fire broke out.

———————

I made general small talk and told her about my new interest in genealogy. With trepidation, I brought up the topic of slavery. "Oh, yes, the Kilby's owned slaves, but I never really looked into it." So, I started to show her my research and all the slave names I had found.

When I came to the name Simon, Aunt Lucia took on a quizzical look. "Hmm, that name sounds familiar." She disappeared into another room. (Her house was filled with antiques from her family and the Kilbys.) She brought back a very old-looking crockery jar, reached in, and pulled out a note. It was written by my Aunt Marie, who used to live in Mont Medi before Aunt Lucia and Uncle Billy. The note read: "Uncle Simon Kilby's Pickle Jar. Buster got this jar from him. Mama gave it to me."

Uncle Simon Kilby's pickle jar.

Aunt Lucia did not know who Buster was, but "Mama" was my grandmother. Wasn't this the Simon Kilby I had been researching? We had no White Simon's in our family tree. And it was customary to call older slaves and former slaves "Uncle."

I took photos of the jar, and then gently asked if I could have the jar or purchase it from her. I was hoping to be able to give it to Betty. But Aunt Lucia did not want to part with it. It was quite the gift anyway, just to see and hold this jar. I felt like I was holding history.

Note inside Uncle Simon Kilby's pickle jar.

My scientific self knew that I had no proof that this was Juliet's Simon. But I had searched the entire Rappahannock,

Madison, and Culpeper county censuses for many decades after 1870 and never found another, except Simon and Lucy Frances' son, Simeon, Jr. He was six years old in 1900 and appears to have died before 1910. In my bones, I feel this pickle jar belonged to Simon Kilby, Juliet's son.

After I showed my photos to Betty, she felt it also. Then we had an intriguing conversation about pickles, because both our families made them. For both of us, it was a rare lunch or dinner that did not include homemade pickles. We compared the kinds of pickles our families made, and they seemed like the same kinds from the same recipes. Another connection!

Still, with all my research, I did not have proof that Betty was related to Juliet's son, Simon Kilby. I went to the archives at the Library of Virginia in Richmond where I spent hours looking at microfilms of birth and death records. The microfilm reels had been created in the 1970s. The photography of the records was poor quality, and the films were very dirty. Just about the time I scrolled through and found something promising, a big glob of dirt would get in the way. I found some records of the births of Simon and Lucy Frances' children, including a son (no name given) born in 1882. That could have been John Henry, Betty's grandfather. Perhaps I could find a record of John Henry's death. I knew from a headstone in a Rappahannock County cemetery that John Henry had died on September 25, 1958.

A helpful archivist told me that the death records for that period had yet to be photographed and archived. I would need to go to the Division of Vital Statistics of the Virginia Department of Health to find the death certificate.

It would be an all-day affair. I drove 2½ hours to Richmond, found the Division of Vital Statistics, and then completed a long application form requesting John Henry Kilby's death certificate. I filled out one for his wife Ella also. The clerk told me that it could take up to four hours for her staff to find and copy the records for me. The waiting room was filled with people, all requesting records.

I walked around downtown Richmond, looking at all the historic buildings and monuments, most of them Confederate. The last hour was excruciating, but finally my name was called. I was trembling as I took the papers in my hands. A quick read, and "Eureka"—the answers were all there! John Henry Kilby's father was Simon Kilby and his mother, Fannie Wallace. They were Betty's great-grandparents!

Please don't think that I was interested only in the men in the family. I also researched the women, looking for more information on Juliet, her mother Sarah, Simon's wife Fannie, and John Henry's wife Mary Ella. I gained so many insights about the hardships of slavery and Jim Crow. While they were struggling, the women in my White family had slaves to help them on the family farms where they lived. These White women did have very large families, usually six to 10 children, and so lived most of their lives pregnant and taking care of children. They probably needed these children to help on their farms. But I think they had it far better than their African American slaves and neighbors.

With the discovery that Betty was truly descended from people my family enslaved (see pages 66 and 67), I slowed down my research. I wanted to focus more on developing a relationship with Betty and her family. I was feeling called to do whatever I could to make amends for how they had been treated by my family. I also wanted to explore my own role in the oppression of African Americans and how I had benefitted in life by being White.

Betty Kilby's Family Tree (Simplified*)
(As of September 2020)

* Additional information: www.acommongrace.org/genealogy

2000

1900

1800

1700

James M.
Kilby

John F.
Kilby

Betty Ann
Kilby (Baldwin)

Patricia
Kilby - Robb

Gene M.
Kilby

James
Wilson
Kilby

Catherine
Ausberry

John
Henry
Kilby

Mary
Ella
Kilby

Simon
Kilby

Lucy F. Wallace

John
Kilby

James
Kilby

Sarah
Kilby

Child (Male)

Child (Male)

Juliet Ann
(_____)

Adult
(Male)

Celia
(_____)

Sarah
(_____)

?
Henry
(_____)

Enslaved by
Thomas & Malinda
Kilby

Enslaved by
Leroy & Sarah
Kilby

In a way, I handed the task of continuing the genealogical work to my cousin Tim. Tim heard about what I was doing and contacted me. He had been doing genealogical research on our family for years and had found some of the same information I had found. He was interested in expanding the research on both the White and Black Kilbys.

Tim and I had not seen each other for 40 years, since our grandmother's funeral. I introduced him to Betty and her brother James, and Tim started to come to some of Betty's and my presentations. He attended James's installation as pastor of the First Baptist Church of Washington (Virginia), a day-long affair where Tim and I were introduced to the pomp and circumstance of the African American Church.

Tim is an expert and tireless genealogical researcher. He has spent far more hours that I ever did at the Library of Virginia and been far more creative in accessing a wide array of resources. For example, he has found and utilized church records, military records, the U.S. Find a Grave Index, Social Security Applications/Claims, City Directories, WPA Slave Narratives, correspondence, farm ledgers, newspapers, and books and magazines. His research has taken him all across Virginia and into other states as members of Betty's family migrated out of Virginia. As a result, he has filled out the roots and crown of Betty's family tree so that it is a mighty monarch. He is documenting this in a book to be entitled *Gourdvine Black and White*. It tells the stories of three generations of African American Kilbys, those of Sarah, Juliet, and Juliet's children, and their relationships to the White Kilbys.

Tim's research has filled in some important gaps in my research. One amazing find was a deed to settle ownership of land from Charles W. Kilby's estate. In the deed, it states that Charles W. Kilby was also known as Simon Kilby and is the same person. That mystery is solved. Lucy Frances did not remarry. I like to think that Simon threw off the name given him by his enslavers and chose another one! Good for him!

Simon Kilby, Betty's great-grandfather.

Tim somehow found a photo of Simon Kilby, too. He becomes a real person before us now, so friendly looking and dignified.

Tim also discovered the possible connection between Betty's family and the Finks family. It certainly is convoluted, but it makes some sense. Malinda Kilby's second husband Bluford Thornhill, whom she married in 1865, had a daughter Sarah Ann by his previous marriage. Sarah Ann married P.M. Finks. It appears that after emancipation, Simon ended up working for P.M. Finks, the one who wrote the consent note for Simon's marriage.

We still do not know who Simon's father was. There were no male slaves in the household when Juliet was having her children. Betty thinks that the father was probably Mortimer Kilby, who sued his mother for ownership of Juliet and the children in 1865. But Mortimer's brothers were also in the household.

Tim has some ideas about this, based on DNA matching technology. He has become an expert in DNA analysis for genealogical purposes. As he was discovering and connecting with more and more African American Kilbys, he met a second cousin of Betty's. This person, who shall remain anonymous, was willing to have his DNA tested. The results came in in 2016. Tim and this person share a common ancestor, James Kilby, Mortimer's grandfather. So, Betty and I really are cousins! She knew it all along.

Tim's DNA analysis points to Mortimer's brother James Franklin as the possible father of Simon, based on other White Kilby DNA tests registered online. He served as his mother Malinda's overseer. But there can be mutations over the generations that make DNA analysis imperfect. Mortimer could be the father, as could my great-grandfather Andrew Jackson Kilby or one of his brothers. They all lived in the vicinity. Juliet's children could have had different fathers. But what we know is that Juliet was violated by one or more of the White Kilbys. We need to make amends for this violation, if that is even possible.

Few of the old Kilby farms remain in the family's ownership (I know of only one), and of course, as land is sold, it can be divided and combined into different plots. But because the areas of Culpeper, Rappahannock, and Madison counties where my family lived have remained so rural, the plots have remained remarkably similar to what they were.

My Aunt Lucia took me to visit the farms of my great-great-grandfather Leroy and great-grandfather Andrew Jackson. The cemeteries located on these old farms contain their graves. The gravestones of Andrew Jackson and his wife Ellen lay in a pasture, the stones knocked over by the cows.

———————

Tim has spent hours poring over deeds of land owned by our ancestors. He has been able to identify land owned by Malinda Kilby during the time that she and her husband Thomas owned Juliet and her mother Sarah. Contacting the current owner, Tim visited the site in 2019. The owner said, yes, he knew that the land had once been owned by Kilbys and directed Tim to a place where there was evidence of an old house. It was just stone and brick rubble.

As Tim was walking around, an old brick lying on the ground caught his eye. He picked it up, and there was a distinct human handprint pressed into the clay. It appears to belong to a woman, based on its size. Tim calculates that the house would have been built when Thomas was alive, perhaps after he purchased Sarah, Juliet's mother. Could this be Sarah's handprint? Slaves, even women, were often enlisted in building projects. Tim is currently doing more research on the age of the brick, but Betty and I like to think of it as "Sarah's Brick." Maybe it is, maybe it isn't.

The owner of the land kindly gave Tim the brick, and he showed it to me and Betty in November 2019. Betty laid her hand on the print, and it fit perfectly.

Brick found on property of Malinda Kilby. "Sarah's brick," named for Sarah, great-great-great-grandmother of Betty Kilby Baldwin.

THE FOREVER FIGHT

10

BETTY AND PHOEBE

Phoebe: Soon after meeting Betty's family, I started reading the book that Betty's brother James Kilby had written, *The Forever Fight*. He also tells the story of integrating Warren County High School, but from a different perspective. He was the oldest child, a boy, who had to be the leader and pioneer. He was the first in his family to attend that regional public boarding school for "Colored children," because

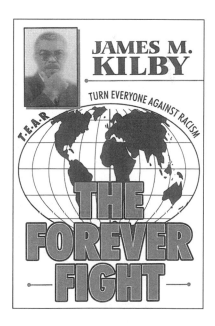

Warren County had no high school for African Americans.

He tells of not getting enough food to last the weekend and the water pipes freezing in the winter. That meant no water to drink or to bathe. Boys would file down pennies to the size of dimes so they could afford a Coke from the machine. James caught a bad cold, and by the end of the year he had lost so much weight that he weighed less than 80 pounds. That's why his father insisted that he and his brother John be allowed to attend another school—a "Colored" high school located in another county, but only a half-hour drive from Front Royal.

His father arranged for a public school bus to take them to and from that school every day. One evening it was snowing, and the bus slid off the road on the way home. It took hours for another bus to be secured, so the kids arrived home after 9:00 pm. When James told me the story later, he reminded me that there were no cell phones then. They had to flag down a car and get that person to call the school offices when they got home. There was no way to tell parents what was going on, so the parents were worried sick. Of course, Mr. Kilby did not want James—or Betty or John—to go through another year like that.

BETTY: I can hardly bear to remember those days when Jimmy was away from us in school. Especially the stories he would tell on the weekends when he came home. I just could not figure out where I wanted to go to school when I finished 7th grade.

PHOEBE: James' description of integrating Warren County High School mirrors yours, Betty, although he wasn't there as long. That did not make it easier, just mercifully shorter. He graduated in 1961, but soon thereafter, the mud-ball-throwing fracas with the White boys happened. The White boys told the police that the Kilby kids had thrown rocks, so James had to flee to avoid being jailed for assault. He ended up moving to the Washington, D.C. area.

By 1963, he had gotten a job with the CIA and was eventually detailed to the White House. There he served as a courier for several years. This was before fax machines or the internet, so couriers were essential for transporting documents quickly from the White House to Congress, the Supreme Court, and all the other government agencies. James remembers taking copies of President Lyndon Johnson's State of the Union Address document to Congress.

BETTY: Jimmy is a keen observer, and none of these experiences was lost on him, going the whole way back to his suffering as an adolescent at the regional public boarding school. It all led him to a life of activism.

PHOEBE: The man has been dedicated to the cause of justice, even as he worked to support his family. He started an organization called TEAR—"Treat Every American Right." It sponsored a fundraiser to support Frank Wills, the security guard at the Watergate who discovered the tape on the door, placed there by burglars infiltrating the Democratic National Committee (DNC) Headquarters. James had met Mr. Wills when he made deliveries to the DNC. Mr. Wills had fallen on hard times, even though his diligence had led to the discovery of the burglars and eventually to President Richard Nixon's resignation.

Later, James moved to Annapolis, Maryland. He joined others there to form a group called Concerned Black Males. They dedicated themselves to counseling young Black males at Annapolis High School about how to stay out of trouble and about the importance of education. The group also helped resolve disciplinary disputes and then trained student leaders to handle disputes. It sounds like an early form of restorative justice to me. They were even able to organize a trip to China for the boys. With his visit to China, James developed an international message for TEAR—"Turn Everyone Against Racism."

When I met James in 2007, he was living in Front Royal, having moved back to help take care of his elderly parents some years before. If I had contacted Betty and James a few years earlier, I would have had the opportunity to meet their father, but he passed away in 2003.

I guess that I made a good enough impression on James Kilby at that first family dinner I attended so that in 2008, he invited me to a meeting of another activist group he had formed, the Historical Education Movement (HEM). (Betty was still living in Texas, and so could not attend HEM meetings.)

Since the 50th anniversary of the integration of Warren County High School was coming up in February 2009, HEM decided to focus on hosting some major commemorative events. The school board agreed that the big event could take place at the new high school's huge auditorium.

HEM wanted to prepare a quality commemorative program booklet to give to attendees, but the printing would require funding. As a businessperson in the Shenandoah Valley since 1996, I had a fair number of contacts and offered to help James raise advertising dollars for the program. (As I look back on this now, I see that I used my White privilege to assist James and HEM. Good idea or bad?)

I was able to secure meetings with several bank presidents, who purchased ads. James and I were a good team. He described the event, and I made the fundraising pitch.

On February 21, 2009, we filled that auditorium with community members and dignitaries to honor those who had integrated Warren County High. About six of the original 23 African American students were there.

BETTY: I was so excited to see my fellow students—and to have Phoebe and my brother Jimmy working together on the event. Phoebe had become a fighter in her own right. She could get through doors that Jimmy couldn't. We were so happy to have her on our team. This kind of work was truly a fight. When Daddy went to the land of "no mo" (died, passed on, transitioned), Jimmy picked up the baton and continued the fight. I could hardly believe that 50 years had passed.

I was relieved that the 50th Anniversary was being held at the new Skyline High School. The memories were difficult enough to deal with. It was good not to be haunted by the old building's ghosts.

My job was to honor those students who had participated in the integration but were no longer with us. I called each of their names—Barbara Jackson, John Jackson, Louise Dean, Elizabeth Dean, Cuetta Grier, Frank Grier, Archie Pines, and Stephen Travis. We had a prayer for their families and a time of silence. I wondered if the trauma of 50 years ago had anything to do with their early exit from life. By the time I got back to my seat, I wondered why my name wasn't on the list and one of my classmates was doing the tribute instead. Rebecca Fletcher looked over at me and said, "Good job," and I knew it was all God's plan.

PHOEBE: HEM also wanted to tell the story of the integration of Warren County High School to children. We hosted a Candlelight Vigil at WCHS on the exact 50th anniversary day, February 18th, 2009. We placed candles on 23 two-foot high holders along the drive that led from the bottom of the hill to the school building at the top, so that we could recreate the walk up the hill 50 years earlier, but in a safe environment. As we walked up the hill, children attending were invited at each candle to read a remembrance quote for one of the students who integrated the school. I found it moving to see the children and parents so involved in this very simple event.

Program cover for the 50th anniversary of the integration of Warren County High School, February 21, 2009.

CANDLELIGHT VIGIL

FEBRUARY 18, 2009
SIX O'CLOCK

GROUNDS OF THE FORMER
WARREN COUNTY HIGH SCHOOL

PRAYER   REVEREND JAMES M. KILBY

LIGHTING OF THE CANDLES

**READING OF THE NAMES TO HONOR
THE 23 AFRICAN AMERICAN STUDENTS**

MEMORIAL WALK WITH REMEMBRANCES

BENEDICTION   REVEREND ALFRED WOODS

COMMEMORATION

FEBRUARY 21, 2009
ONE O'CLOCK UNTIL THREE O'CLOCK

SKYLINE HIGH SCHOOL

WELCOME   MR. ANDREW KELLER PRINCIPAL, SKYLINE HIGH SCHOOL

INTRODUCTION   YOLONDA W. BROWN

PRAYER   REVEREND CHRISTOF WEBER

MUSICAL SELECTIONS
"HAND ME DOWN MY SILVER TRUMPET" BY JOY WEBB
WARREN COUNTY MIDDLE SCHOOL CHOIR BETH WHITNEY, DIRECTOR

MUSICAL SELECTION
THE ANOINTED VOICES BAYLEN BROOKS, DIRECTOR

"TREASURE EACH MOMENT" BY JOSEPH M. MARTIN
"LET THERE BE PEACE" BY ANDY BECK
WARREN COUNTY HIGH SCHOOL AND SKYLINE HIGH SCHOOL CHOIRS
JAMIE DEAN-BRACKETT AND TOM BOWEN, DIRECTORS

**HISTORY AND SIGNIFICANCE OF THE
INTEGRATION OF WARREN COUNTY HIGH SCHOOL**
PATRICK FARRIS EXECUTIVE DIRECTOR, WARREN HERITAGE SOCIETY

**PRESENTATIONS BY PARTICIPANTS IN THE
INTEGRATION OF WARREN COUNTY HIGH SCHOOL**

MUSICAL SELECTION
THE ANOINTED VOICES BAYLEN BROOKS, DIRECTOR

INTRODUCTION OF JACK W. GRAVELY   REVEREND ALFRED WOODS

COME TOGETHER WITH YOUR COMMUNITY JACK W. GRAVELY

MUSICAL SELECTIONS
"A CHANGE IS GONNA COME" BY SAM COOKE
JOHN "BO" FLYNN, SOLOIST
THE ANOINTED VOICES BAYLEN BROOKS, DIRECTOR

BENEDICTION   REVEREND ALLEN BALTIMORE

But HEM was not finished with its work. The group hoped to have the old high school, which was now being renovated into a middle school, named after James's and Betty's father. This would be fitting, since it is the building that was actually integrated by the Kilby family in 1959. We held strategy meetings at Williams Chapel, the same location where Attorney

Phoebe leads children in Candlelight Vigil, February 18, 2009.

parents and children during the integration period. We honed our arguments and wrote letters to the editor. We printed T-shirts so that when we went to school board meetings, they could see how many there supported naming the school James Wilson Kilby Middle School.

But some others in the community opposed our proposal. One person wrote a letter to the editor in favor of naming the school after the WCHS principal at the time who supported the Whites-only system. After several public hearings and meetings where HEM was present in full force, the school board decided to name the school Warren County Middle School. We were all disappointed, but James was truly discouraged.

———◆———

The Town Council of Front Royal, however, was paying attention. They had no control over the Warren County School

Board, but they did control the streets of the town where the school was located. They notified James that they would rename a short street on one side of the school property "Kilby Drive." James looks happy in the photo, and he truly appreciated what the town did. He told me after the ceremony that he couldn't help but think that this was just a consolation prize.

James M. Kilby at the dedication of Kilby Drive, Front Royal, VA.

BETTY: HEM did not meet for a while after the school board defeat. But then Phoebe and Jimmy came up with the idea to host a community-wide dialogue to begin the process of healing wounds from racial conflicts within the town of Front Royal and Warren County. This is long-term work that demands persistence!

PHOEBE: We held six dialogues to share perspectives and stories about the history of integrating the local public schools and that action's impact on current community racial understanding and integration in general.

Our planning committee enlisted a cross-section of the community. Nineteen people agreed to join the dialogue after we contacted more than 50. It is difficult to entice people to do this work. The community still suffers deep wounds from the Massive Resistance era. Some people don't want to think and talk about what happened. Fears, resentments, and jealousies over who deserves credit or attention, anger, and hurts remain.

And we were asking for a big commitment of time. But we did find 19 who were ready to talk.

The 19 represented many types of people:

- African Americans who were the first to integrate Warren County High School (James and Betty Kilby, and Matthew Pines; Betty could only attend a few sessions, because she had to travel from Texas.)
- African Americans who chose to attend the all-Black Criser School
- African Americans who attended Warren County High School in later years
- Bo Flynn, the African American bus driver during the era

BETTY: He slowed down our bus so we Black students could figure out our school safety plans on the way to school each morning! (See page 48.)

PHOEBE: Others in the group of 19 who agreed to participate in the dialogues were—

- African American members of the local community today, who belonged to the Historical Education Movement (HEM)
- Whites who attended Warren County High School as the Class of 1959, but could not graduate because the school was closed by the governor during Massive Resistance
- A White person who attended the all-White private school, Mosby Academy
- A White teacher at Warren County High School during the era

- White members of the local community today, who belonged to HEM
- Two current Assistant Superintendents of Schools in Warren County

With grant money, we hired two trained outside facilitators, one African American, Carlyle Victor, and one European American, Belinda Reed, to help us with our later dialogues. Both were trained and skilled in restorative justice and used a circle process for our dialogue.

We sat in a circle and passed around a talking piece, as one by one we expressed our thoughts and feelings and shared stories and points of view. To make the sessions more meaningful and healing, we opened and closed the sessions with various types of rituals, including poems, songs, and prayers. It was especially moving when Bo Flynn, the bus driver, sang his special version of the classic 1964 song "A Change is Gonna Come" by popular singer-song writer, Sam Cooke. Bo had sung this at the 50th Anniversary Commemoration of the integration of Warren County High School, and it continued to inspire us during these conversations.

We planned a series of dialogue questions, though as you can imagine, these changed over time as the group got to know each other.

Here is what we ended up discussing:

- Why did you decide to join this dialogue?
- Who else should be involved in this dialogue?
- What was your experience of racial integration in your school and community during your high school years?

- How does having experienced racial integration in your school and community during your high school years affect you now?
- How does what happened affect the Front Royal community now?
- What should we do next:
  - to bring our shared history to light?
  - to bring healing to our community? (Create a list of ideas as an action plan.)
- If our goals are to raise awareness of the history and to foster community healing, what benefits does each idea offer, and what challenges?
- Which ideas are the most important for meeting our goals? (We included a voting exercise to help set priorities for ideas in the action plan.)
- Are you willing to work on the action plan after this dialogue is over?

You might think that this was all very organized and went as outlined, progressing from one question to the next. But our conversations definitely veered here and there, with emotions becoming high at times.

People tended to be polite and tried to avoid conflict, but now and then differences broke through and honest discussion ensued. One such moment happened early on, when the question of what we should call ourselves came up: White? Black? African American? European American? Some insisted that only "African American" should be used. Others said that "Black" was okay. No one seemed to like "European American," so we ended up with "African American" and "White."

Things got hot about using the word "nigger," when referring to an historical event or incident. One African American objected to White people saying the word. It made him uncomfortable. Then a White participant pointed out that an African American had used the term already in the dialogue. We ran out of time before all this was resolved, but from then on, participants avoided using "nigger." We had expressed ourselves, and we knew each other's sensitivities.

Another tense moment came when an African American suggested that the Warren County School Board should issue an apology. The White man who had attended the Whites-only private school (Mosby Academy) during the integration period became very upset and objected vigorously. Tensions in the room were high.

BETTY: I understood how this man felt. The White children felt that we forced them out of their school. They felt hurt because their lives were disrupted, too. The White woman who got up at my presentation at the Historical Society had talked about how we disrupted *everybody*'s life. I knew there were families where the mother wanted the children to go to WCHS and the father wanted the children to go to Mosby, so there were conflicts within families. The children were exposed to this conflict. Best friends were separated and couldn't graduate together.

In our conversations, we were putting the focus on the African American children's experiences, and this man wanted the group to know that he felt pain, too. He was sitting in the circle directly across from me; I couldn't help but make eye contact. I got up, walked over to him, put my arms around him, and hugged him. I could feel him dropping the rocks. This was that empathy bond of love that I had learned from my study of the Beloved Community.

PHOEBE: Gradually, the group built up a level of trust so that we could work together to develop a plan of action for addressing the harms of Massive Resistance. For the last two sessions, as we developed our plan, we participated in a ritual of building a cairn of Shenandoah River rocks. Each person thought of someone who did the right thing during the integration era, someone who was a model, a beacon leading us in the way forward. Each participant chose a rock symbolizing that person, and then placed that stone on the cairn and named the person. The cairn was to remind us of the right path, just as cairns are used to mark walking paths in rough terrain around the world.

Cairn built by our "Shared History" dialogue group.

We each came up with our list of possible next steps and used a voting process to decide our priorities. Here are the top 10 ideas with many tie votes. The final vote was unanimous to adopt this action plan, even though it included an apology. Betty had won him over.

PRIORITY 1:

- Ensure support for a Virginia historical highway marker for the former Warren County High School.

PRIORITY 2:

- Create a student-friendly resource center on the desegregation era history of Warren County, including a documentary film and website.

PRIORITY 3:
- Create a speaker's bureau for schools and public events.
- Create opportunities for reconciliation/apology.

PRIORITY 4:
- Collect and archive photos and documents of the Massive Resistance period and its aftermath.
- Issue a news release by HEM (Historical Education Movement) and this group and inform the public about the "Brown vs. Board of Education" scholarship fund.
- Host a public dialogue/discussion on TV. Invite public figures to participate.
- In 2011, host a commemoration of the 50th anniversary of the graduation of the first integrated class at Warren County High School in 1961. Invite Mosby Academy (all-White private school) Class of 1961.

PRIORITY 5:
- Ask/press hard for the Warren County School Board or Board of Supervisors to express profound regret or apology for Warren County's role in Massive Resistance/ unequal educational opportunities and facilities.
- Commemorate Criser High School and other sites important to the era.

Around this time, the Virginia Department of Historic Resources developed a program to highlight the Civil Rights Era in Virginia and honor all the people who were involved in the five school integration cases during Massive Resistance. They held ceremonies in Richmond for Betty, James, and the others.

Unveiling of the Historic Marker in front of the historic Warren County High School, June 8, 2011.

The department realized that their historical markers in Virginia offered a lopsided picture of Virginia history, most of them describing the homes of founding fathers or Civil War battles. When we contacted them about a marker to be placed in front of WCHS, the staff was eager to support the effort. James spoke to Lou Justis,

Virginia Department of Historic Resources Marker.

the Assistant Superintendent of Schools who had participated in all the dialogue sessions, and together they were able to get the school board to approve paying for the cost of the marker.

But then came the matter of deciding the exact wording on the sign. The word limit was approximately 100 words. HEM's wording focused on Massive Resistance. But the school board wanted to include information about the school's architecture and how its construction was funded by the New Deal Public Works Administration.

The Department of Historic Resources had the final say on the text and agreed that the focus should be on School Integration and Massive Resistance. On June 8, 2011, the community, school board, and Virginia Department of Historic Resources dedicated the sign.

Warren County High School and Massive Resistance

Warren County High School, a Public Works Administration project, was constructed in 1940. In 1958, the local NAACP chapter, led by James W. Kilby, won a federal suit against the Warren County School Board to admit African Americans for the first time. In response, Gov. James Lindsay Almond Jr. ordered it closed in Sept. 1958, the first school in Virginia shut down under the state's Massive Resistance strategy. Following the 1959 Virginia Supreme Court of Appeals ruling that Massive Resistance was unconstitutional, the U. S. Circuit Court ordered it reopened. On 18 Feb. 1959, 23 African American students walked up this hill and integrated the school.

James and I served on the planning committee for the event. James had already been selected to offer the invocation and give an address. I asked Betty if she would be willing to give the benediction and lead the crowd up the hill to the school for the reception afterwards. She said yes. The planning committee approved.

But Betty and I talked about something else. I asked her if, when the group walked up the hill, she would be willing to take the hand of one of the white students and walk in through the school doors together? She liked the symbolism and agreed this would be a good idea. When she and others took hands, the local TV news station filmed the moment and broadcast it and the story to the community that evening.

Soon thereafter, the school board mandated including the history of the integration of WCHS and Massive Resistance in the school curriculum for 3rd, 7th, and 11th grades. James was

James Kilby speaks to a third grade class about school integration history at A.S. Rhodes Elementary School, Front Royal, VA.

asked to speak in classrooms, giving these presentations for several years.

After the marker dedication, James decided he needed a break. He had been involved in the "Forever Fight," well, forever. I, Phoebe, really wanted to continue working on the other parts of "Our Shared History" plan, but it was not my place to forge ahead without James. This is his history and his fight.

Without James, HEM disbanded, though there are still activists in the Front Royal area who continue to fight for racial equity. Betty and I would meet up with them many years later amid another controversy. James soon became pastor of First Baptist Church of Washington, Virginia, and now preaches as guest minister in other churches.

BETTY: We take our children, grandchildren, friends, family—and anyone interested in our story—to Kilby Street, the former Warren County High School, and the road marker as we talk about the historical movement that has happened in Front Royal, Virginia. Another degree of healing is taking place. "Truth and Mercy have met together; Peace and Justice have kissed."

SOJOURNER TRUTH IN KALAMAZOO

11

BETTY

DADDY DIED MAY 2, 2003, at age 85. I wanted him to see my book, *Wit, Will & Walls*, but I didn't want him to ever know the price we children had to pay for our education.

I sensed that he was in his final days, so I had the printer make a single copy of the book's front and back covers and first chapter. Then I gave it to him and read from the chapter. We laughed and we cried together. He wanted the world to know the importance of the Warren County case and its impact on public education, so I wrote the book to fulfill his wish.

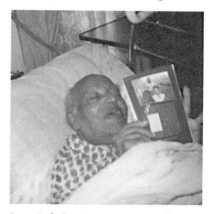

Betty's father, James Wison Kilby, in his nursing home, reading Betty's book, *Wit, Will & Walls*.

He watched my first TV interview. I had taken a copy of the interview to the nursing home and showed it on the TV in the lobby so his caregivers and fellow residents could see it, too. The interview ended with a picture of Daddy and me, and then closed in on Daddy so that he covered the entire screen. Everyone congratulated him and wanted to shake his hand. One guy yelled, "Oh Kilby, you are going to be famous." Daddy had the biggest grin on his face.

He was so happy that at last the story of his fight for his children's education would reach a larger audience. Daddy had the wisdom to realize that no matter how much it hurt, the truth had to be told. He believed that the history was as important as the education he wanted for us. I knew he was pleased that I hadn't let the story be buried.

A month after his death, I was on a book tour telling people why he fought so hard and sacrificed so much to get his children educated. I didn't realize at the time that I was still grieving losing him, and grieving the pain of trying to be able to go to an integrated school. When I started giving presentations, I told the story in third person to avoid being emotionally overwhelmed. At the end I would announce, "If you haven't guessed by now, I am that little girl and this is my story." Each time, I felt that little girl's pain. I had avoided the Kilby name for so long, I had to learn to write Betty Kilby Fisher when autographing books. When I got home from giving presentations, I stayed in my pajamas until my heart and soul healed from constantly reliving the trauma. I was on a mission to make Daddy proud of me by fulfilling his dream. I sensed his spirit was with me.

It took me six months to realize that traditional marketing strategies weren't working for me. I was failing. I would travel to do book signings at bookstores, but I barely made enough sales to pay my expenses. I wasn't paid for most of the presentations. Nearly a year after the book was published, I did my first signing at a military base and had my first of many $1,000 sales days. With a little money in the bank, I could launch a good marketing campaign and sell the book at conferences. The contacts I made at conferences often led to paid speaking opportunities and radio and TV interviews. Every time I was paid to speak, I asked my host to arrange for me to speak at a local high school. I preferred the school with the greatest need.

2004 was the 50th anniversary of Brown v. Board of Education. One student told me her teacher taught her that the only thing she needed to remember was "1954, segregation no more." Many students thought this was something that happened only in Topeka, Kansas. Lawyers and legal professionals studied Brown v. Board and they knew it involved five

Betty and her grandson Eric Jones selling *Wit, Will & Walls*.

cases. But very few people knew our family's story. Some of the individuals who were part of the more widely publicized Brown cases called me a stepchild when I appeared at some of the 50th Anniversary commemorations of Brown. John Stokes was the exception.

John was involved in the student strike that led to the Prince Edward County case in Farmville, Virginia, another one of the five Brown v. Board cases. We often presented together as the "Author and Finisher of Desegregation in Virginia."

The King Commission in Richmond, Virginia, was charged with the responsibility of coordinating the events for the 50th Anniversary of Brown v. Board. I was invited to become a member of the Commission. My living in Texas and having to fly to Richmond monthly at my own expense was a costly yet valuable connection. It gave me access to some good opportunities.

I was invited to speak at the Hart-Dole Federal Center in Battle Creek, Michigan, and was excited not only about the assignment, but also because the city has a museum with a Sojourner Truth exhibit. She is one of my heroes who gives me inspiration to carry on in difficult times.

The Sojourner Truth Monument was within walking distance of my hotel. My heart pounded as I stood next to the 12-foot-high sculpture of the woman.

I read, "It's up to us who walk in Sojourner Truth's footsteps to carry on into the future and continue to build upon her legacy," Velma Laws Clay. I was embarrassed about how I could whimper and whine about my own journey as I stood in front of this extraordinary African American woman.

I wonder how one goes on when your children are sold into slavery as hers were? I cannot imagine the pain. How did that not kill her spirit? What can the activist in me learn from Sojourner, the activist?

There at the statue, feeling like I was in the presence of Sojourner Truth herself, I confessed that when I sat in Dr. Hofstra's Virginia History class, I didn't want to study history because it meant talking about slavery. Yet from Dr. Hofstra I learned about the free Black community that developed in the midst of slavery. I had never heard about it before. I learned that the first Africans who came to America as indentured servants, lived out their period of indentureship and helped formulate the free Negro community. Dr. Hofstra even taught that my case was an important part of history. But I didn't want to learn more about my people's history because it hurt, and everything that I already knew didn't do a thing to make me feel good about myself. I would rather have been ignorant of my history than become better informed because of the pain involved.

Dr. Hofstra managed to get me to open my eyes to my ancestors and the great accomplishments that they made, despite suffering and sacrifice. And that day, before the towering statue, I picked up my father's dream. I recognized that Sojourner Truth and so many of my ancestors laid the foundation for me to go on and do great things. I accepted the baton on behalf of future generations. I want them to be able to look back and see the foundation laid for them by Sojourner Truth—and even Betty Kilby.

That evening, I felt like I fully connected with people during the TV interview and the library book signing. At the presentation the next day, I was able to tell the story of "Desegregation in Virginia." In *first* person.

I spent the final day in Michigan at a school in Kalamazoo. I remembered that the pot-bellied stove at my Colored elementary school had "KALAMAZOO" written on its front. I thought Kalamazoo was such an interesting word, and I remembered the warmth from the stove on this cold winter day. The school didn't have an auditorium or a gym, so my presentations would be to small groups in the library. I started at 7:00 in the morning. The room was filled with dignitaries.

One of the persons attending was active in the NAACP. He contacted someone on the staff of *Crisis Magazine* (the NAACP publication), and the next thing I knew, they were doing an article about my story. I saw it as an opportunity to give a tribute to my dad. A photographer took so many pictures that I began to feel guilty. Daddy should be here. I was carrying on his mission. So I posed in front of a portrait of him. That picture of Daddy and me became a full page in *Crisis Magazine*.

Photo of Betty with her father's photo in the background, which appeared with an article in NAACP's *Crisis Magazine*.

My time with Sojourner Truth had cleared my mind and strengthened my heart. My task was not just to live out Daddy's dream or my dream, but to let today's generation of school-age children know that a long time ago, children fought and sacrificed to make sure they would have equal access to a quality education.

Back to the high school in Kalamazoo—most of the students were African American. I presented to seven student groups throughout the day. Attending my presentations was on a volunteer basis.

The first two groups were responsive. Word got around the school that there was a woman in school that day who was a real part of history. In the third group, when I called for questions, a young man stood up and said, "Mrs. Fisher, before you came today, I thought that stuff was just something we read in history books. Now, I know it's real."

As quickly as he got up, he sat back down, and the students began to clap. It was hard to control my excitement as the students asked questions and I answered.

"Were you afraid?" and I answered, "Yes, I was afraid, but I was brought up in Sunday School and I knew God was with me."

"How come this is the first we are hearing about you?"

I answered, "If it's not in the history books, the whole story isn't being taught. My education about my own history didn't start until I was in college. When I learned one new piece of information about my history, I began to research and look for more. We have Black History Month. You should go to every Black History program you can, and you will find us talking about the accomplishments of African Americans. You have Sojourner Truth right here in your back yard. I visited Sojourner yesterday because I, too, needed to be inspired."

"How come you don't hate White people?"

"When you study your history, you'll learn there were a lot of White people who risked their lives in the Underground Railroad. There were a lot of White people who marched with Dr. King. To bring it closer to home, there were some White people who contributed to helping me and our group of 23 go to school in Washington, D.C., when my local high school was closed. Bottom line, it is not right for me to hate people because of the color of their skin any more than it is right for people to hate me because of the color of my skin.

"My first grandson, whom I love with all my heart, is half White. I can't separate his blood so I can love only the African American part of him. Love and hate can't live together. If you must hate something, hate injustice.

"Read. I am leaving books for the school library. Check them out and read the entire story. I can only hit the highlights in 30 minutes."

The rest of the presentations throughout the day were as dynamic as the third period presentation.

In the last period, I spoke to parents and teachers. One mother said, "I am here to buy the book. I have been trying to get my son to read. He called me today and asked me to come and buy him this book. I had to meet the woman who accomplished in such a short time, the very thing I have been working for years to accomplish."

I left books and a spreadsheet that I called, "Brown X," that tells the Virginia story from Brown V. Board on May 17, 1954 to the 1964 Civil Rights Act.

When I was dropped off back at the airport, I felt good. I received as much as I gave. Dr. King said if we can just help one individual along life's journey, then our living shall not be in vain.

COMMUNING WITH THE ANCESTORS

PHOEBE

12

WHAT WERE THEY thinking?

Why did they think it was acceptable to enslave people, and by that very fact, traumatize and abuse them? How could they look in the eyes of human beings and treat them like animals? How does one convince oneself that it is moral to put your economic needs above the human rights of others?

I contemplate these questions often as I think about my family and what "coming to the table" is all about. In my opinion, the truth-telling part of the journey requires that descendants of enslavers own up to the fact that their family committed atrocities.

Certainly my family treated enslaved persons like property. My great-grandparents Leroy and Sarah enslaved what appears to be a whole family—a man, woman, and two young children—in 1830. But by 1840, the father and one son were gone. It seems likely to me that they were sold. Though they could have been rented out or taken sick and died.

Leroy's brother Thomas purchased Sarah at an estate sale, where eight slaves were sold. Was she stripped away from her family? It seems probable.

Mortimer, Thomas's son, sued his mother Malinda to have the enslaved persons, part of Thomas's estate, divided up among the heirs. In the suit, he talks about Juliet's and her children's value: "These slaves have been raised by said Melinda until the eldest has got to be a boy that could render some service. They are all valuable." It seems to me that it was all about the money.

A fiction is often repeated by Southerners that slaves were better off under the protection of the White masters, because they were incapable of taking care of themselves. Ta-Nehisi Coates, an acclaimed author and journalist who writes about cultural, social, and political issues, particularly regarding African Americans and White supremacy, thinks differently. In his first novel, *The Water Dancer,* he tells the story of a slave, Hiram, who becomes a conductor on the Underground Railroad. While still a slave, Hiram comments: "The masters could not bring water to a boil, harness a horse, nor strap on their own drawers without us. We were better than them—we had to be."

Why, of course, I thought. Enslavers relied on slaves for all or most of their needs. The enslavers did not plant the corn or preserve the foods or make their clothes. The slaves did; they were the ones who knew the most about what was needed for survival. That is why they were so valuable, as Mortimer says.

I recalled passages in Betty's book, *Wit, Will & Walls,* where she describes growing up on the farm with her family and how they were able to live off the land, skills they probably learned from their enslaved ancestors.

"When the apples, cherries, and peaches were in season, we ate fruit until we were sick. We processed and canned the fruit for the winter, never wasting anything. We did the same with the garden vegetables. Sometimes there was so much food, we would share with the neighbors. The work seemed to be never ending. We grew practically everything we ate.

"When we threshed wheat, we would keep a portion of the wheat and have the wheat ground into flour for breads, pastries, and gravies. When we grew corn, besides eating corn-on-the-cob, canning corn, and storing corn for feeding the cows, chickens, and hogs, we would have a portion of the corn ground into cornmeal for corn bread. The chickens produced eggs that we exchanged at the local grocery store for coffee, sugar, and a few other things that we could not grow on the farm. We butchered at least one hog and one cow every year."

I am amazed at Betty's family's self-sufficiency. They certainly could take care of themselves.

Many Southerners also like to think that the slave masters treated their slaves well. When I was in Richmond once with Betty at a ceremony where she and her brother James were being honored for their bravery while integrating their high school, I was talking to an older gentleman afterwards. I told him that my family had once enslaved Betty's and James's. He said in a very patrician Richmond drawl, "Well I am sure that they were good to their slaves." I told him that I was not sure at all about that. He quickly turned to speak to someone else. I don't think he wanted to hear it.

In order to make the slaves do the work demanded, did my family grossly abuse them? By that I mean beat, mutilate, rape, and terrorize them. I have no specific records to prove one way or the other. But then again, the records do show that Juliet had four children while enslaved. There were no male slaves in the household. And we know from DNA testing that Juliet's descendants have White Kilby DNA in them. It seems likely that one or more of the White Kilbys raped Juliet. One would like to think that there was some more positive relationship, even love, but that is wishful thinking. It was probably an economic decision. If Juliet had children, that added to the wealth of the enslavers' household. I find it hard to say this because this is my family, but this is evidence of gross abuse.

———•———

I have also thought about the women enslavers and how they might have treated their slaves. Sarah and Juliet were enslaved many years by Malinda Kilby after her husband's death in 1834, Juliet from her birth until emancipation in 1865. Did Malinda look the other way, when Juliet became pregnant and pretend it was not one of her sons? How did she treat Juliet and her children? Again, I have discovered no records describing how Juliet and her children were treated by Malinda. I have had to resort to other accounts to speculate.

The book, *They Were Her Property: White Women as Slave Owners in the American South,* by Stephanie E. Jones-Rogers, offers some insights. The author draws on slave narratives, many recorded by the Works Progress Administration (WPA), to learn straight from the slaves how they were treated. There is some evidence of good treatment, or I should say, better than the worst treatment.

For example, Sarah and John Bethea were enslavers in Marion County, South Carolina. She brought to the marriage her own slaves. According to Hester Hunter, one of Sarah's slaves, Sarah treated her slaves differently than her husband treated his. "Sarah's slaves were looked after 'in de right way.' She cared for them when they were ill, made sure they ate well, and had their healthy meals prepared.

"Hunter recalled that her mistress never had the enslaved people she owned 'cut up en slashed up no time'; she 'wouldn' allow no slashin round bout whe' she was,' and she made sure that her husband refrained from punishing her slaves as well." Maybe, Malinda acted similarly.

On the other hand, Jones-Rogers reports that many women abused their slaves, learning their methods from childhood. "According to Henry Watson, his 'mistress had been brought up in Louisiana, and had witnessed punishment all her life, and had become hardened to it.' He had seen her 'perpetrate some of the most cruel acts that a human being could....

"She seemed to take delight in torturing—in fact, she made it a pastime, she inspired every one about her with terror." It hurts to think that Malinda, or my great-grandparents Leroy and Sarah, and other Kilby enslavers, might have acted in this way.

And then there is the Civil War. As a person who values peacebuilding, I avoided exploring this aspect of my family for a long time, in fact, for six years after I first met Betty and her family. My family was not like some Southern families who liked to talk about and praise their Confederate soldier ancestors. I never heard my father speak of them, though he was fond of quoting Robert E. Lee. His favorite Lee maxim was "Deny thyself." He directed this at my sister and me when he thought we were wasteful or asked for too much. I don't like waste, but my father did not exhibit much joy in life. It always felt like he was telling us to deny ourselves joy and happiness.

Why did I finally check out my Confederate ancestors? It is kind of a funny story. Betty, James, and I were scheduled to speak at the Warren Heritage Society in Front Royal, Virginia. We arrived at the building about 40 minutes before the talk was to begin so that we could set up. The Executive Director was supposed to meet us there to unlock the building. Ten minutes went by, then 20 minutes. People started to show up, but none of us could get in the building. One person said, "I think they have a key next door at the Warren Rifles Confederate Museum."

Betty and James looked at me: "Well, we aren't going in there. You will have to fetch the key." I walked over and went in, feeling very uncomfortable. I really did not want to be seen there. The staff person was on the phone and quickly told me that I would have to wait. She talked on and on. The place was festooned with Confederate flags, historic ones and ones for sale.

Meanwhile, an enthusiastic volunteer came over and said, "Are you here to find out about your Confederate ancestors?"

I said, "No, I am just waiting to get the key for the Warren Heritage Society building next door." The woman continued to talk on the phone.

"Well, if you give me the name of an ancestor who might have fought in the war, I can look him up on the computer."

Reluctantly, I said, "Maybe Andrew Jackson Kilby?" He typed in the name. "Why, there are 27 pages of records on him! Do you want to look at them? I could print them out for you."

Oh, no, I thought, I just want to get out of here. Here I was in this Confederate museum talking about my Confederate ancestor, while Betty and James were waiting for me next door for a presentation where I would express regret for my family's participation in slavery. The juxtaposition of opposites was too much. Luckily, the woman finished her phone conversation and handed me the key.

"I'll have to come back later to look at those records."

"You do that!" the volunteer shouted as I walked out the door.

I said to myself, "I am never coming back here." I got someone else to return the key.

I thought about this over the next months. I really should face up to this part of my family heritage, not hide and pretend it didn't happen. It took me about a year, but I finally went back and got the print-out of Andrew Jackson Kilby's records. I also purchased a book detailing the movements and activities of the 7th Virginia Infantry, because I could see that is where Andrew Jackson, known as "Jack," served. The volunteer tried to get me to add a Confederate flag to the purchase, but I declined and got out of there as quickly as I could.

Researching Jack's participation in the Civil War turned out to be fascinating. He was involved in some of the major battles of the Civil War. I had never thought about that. The battles were just lines in a history book before. But Jack was not some major figure. He was a private with the infantry all through the war. So why were there 27 pages of records? Most pages were just photos of single "roll-call" cards giving the month and year and saying he was "Present" or "Absent" or "Sick." But if you look at the book detailing the 7th VA's movements and compare them to Jack's roll-call cards, you can determine where he was and what battles he participated in.

Andrew Jackson Kilby at 25 years old enlisted in the Confederate Army (Company G, the Rappahannock Guard, of the 7th VA Infantry) on May 1, 1861, 17 days after the Battle of Fort Sumter and 14 days after Virginia seceded from the Union. That told me that he did not hesitate to join up; he was an enthusiastic Confederate. By July 17, the 7th VA departed with General Jubal Early's army for McLean's Ford on Bull Run.

It is hard to know whether Jack fought at Bull Run (First Manassas), the first major battle of the war that occurred on July 21, 1861. Early records are not complete. He could have been too sick to fight, because many of the 7th VA were. His roll call card for Jul-Aug 1861, notes that he was discharged from the General Hospital at Culpeper Courthouse on August 22.

Jack seemed to have been sick with "continuing fever" for the rest of 1861, all of 1862, and early 1863. "Continuing fever" was likely typhoid, or maybe malaria. They did not know what it was or how to treat it effectively. While Jack was sick, the 7th VA fought at Yorktown, 2nd Manassas, Sharpsburg, and Fredericksburg.

By May 1863, Jack was ready to rejoin his company, as they passed through Culpeper and headed north to Pennsylvania... to Gettysburg. There Jack participated in the ill-fated "Pickett's Charge" where 6,000 Confederate infantrymen stormed across open fields and fences while Union forces rained down fire from Cemetery Ridge above them. At the end of the fight, more than half of Pickett's Division was dead, wounded, or captured. Jack was wounded.

He survived but did not rejoin the 7th VA until the next year, on February 25, 1864. For the rest of that year, Jack participated in many battles and skirmishes in North Carolina, eventually ending up back in Virginia at Petersburg, defending the Howlett Line earthworks until at least December 1864. After that, the records for Jack stop.

Six Kilbys fought with the 7th VA, including Jack's brother, Henry Clay Kilby. Two of them, Joseph Mortimer and Thomas M., make it all the way to Appomattox, surrendering to the Union on June 28, 1865. Yes, that's the Mortimer Kilby who sued his mother for Juliet and her children.

Soon after putting together this war timeline for Andrew Jackson, I decided that I should visit Gettysburg. My husband and I had been there before, many years ago when I was visiting sites important to my mother's family, who were from Chambersburg and Fayetteville, Pennsylvania, nearby. (My mother's family was River Brethren, a religious group that had an early relationship to the Mennonites. The Mennonites were pacifists. Perhaps that is where I derived my pacifism, though I never spoke to my mother and her family about issues of war and peace.)

I remember from the first visit being annoyed by all the signs and monuments on the Gettysburg battlefield. This time I understood. Map in hand, I could find the exact spot where the 7th VA stood before initiating the charge across the fields toward the Union position on Cemetery Ridge. I could see how impossible it would have been to overtake the Union position and how vulnerable the Confederate troops would have been in their charge.

After visiting this site, we went back to the visitors' center to see the film of the battle. I watched as Pickett's Charge was reenacted. The viewer was on the level of the troops running through the fields with bullets flying and soldiers dropping.

Suddenly, I was overcome by an intense feeling of fear. It was like I was channeling Andrew Jackson, feeling what he felt. I was shaking. The running, the battle, seemed to go on and on. The fear turned into feelings of grief and devastation. I found it hard to look at the screen anymore. I have never felt anything like this before or since. I needed some time to recover from the intense feelings.

I have thought about this a lot since. I don't think that Jack was speaking to me in some way. Instead, my imagination seemed to take over. I am sure that my great-grandfather felt fear, but did he feel grief? The war surely left an indelible imprint on him; his health was damaged by typhoid and wounding. As he lay on his deathbed at the young age of 42, I wonder if he had feelings of regret for having spent his life the way he did.

(There is some evidence that experiencing traumatic events can affect your DNA and that these changes can be passed down to subsequent generations. Andrew Jackson's DNA in me could have triggered this response in my nervous system and caused my strange reactions to the movie, at least in part. The impacts of trauma on the body, nervous system, and DNA are discussed in depth in these two books: *My Grandmother's Hands* by Resmaa Menakem and *The Little Book of Trauma Healing* by Carolyn Yoder. I have since spoken to Carolyn Yoder, and she thinks it is possible that I was experiencing Jack's fear and grief through my DNA and nervous system. I do not know if this is true, but I know that I had those feelings.)

As I think about the enslaving and the warring, it is easy for me—and maybe for you—to get on our high horses and think that we would never do such things. We can easily judge others. But who of us has never done wrong, never made moral compromises to gain economic advantage? When I think of the future and how we all might be judged, I think about how we have contributed to climate change, to subjugating the earth and abusing it. Our descendants might also end up asking: "What were they thinking?"

COMING TO THE TABLE

BETTY AND PHOEBE

COMING TO THE Table (CTTT) began as an idea when Will Hairston and Susan Hutchison started to talk about their heritage as descendants of enslavers. Inspired by Dr. King's dream, they coordinated with the Center for Justice and Peacebuilding at Eastern Mennonite University (EMU) to organize a first gathering of descendants of enslavers and the enslaved at EMU in January 2006. They did not know what might happen and where the gathering might lead.

In the words of one of the participants, Shannon Lanier, a descendant of Thomas Jefferson and Sally Hemmings, "When my cousin Shay Banks-Young, who we call Mama Shay, told me that the descendants of slaves and the descendants of slaveowners were coming together at the 'table of brotherhood' to break bread and to discuss in depth our country's complicated past and its connection to our personal families, I knew I had to be involved. However, I had no idea what to expect.

I'm not even sure if the organization had a mission statement at that point or if they just knew they had a novel idea. Either way, the concept was enough to catch my attention" (*Slavery's Descendants*).

There was no mission statement. There was not an organization. There was just an idea. By the end of the meeting, participants were so inspired that they felt the idea could become a movement and eventually an organization.

It took a while for the movement to get off the ground. Those interested in the idea were scattered across the country, so they had to figure out a way to organize themselves and communicate effectively, something that is difficult without paid staff. The idea needed financial support to become a movement.

While Betty, her brother James, and Phoebe were getting to know each other in 2007 and 2008 by organizing events commemorating school desegregation in Front Royal, Amy Potter of the Center for Justice and Peacebuilding was busy working with CTTT's founders to secure funding from the Fetzer Institute and the Kellogg Foundation. A graduate of the Center for Justice and Peacebuilding, Amy was also developing ideas for applying peacebuilding concepts and skills to create a unique "coming to the table" approach toward racial reconciliation.

In June 2008, she tested these ideas by offering a five-day class, "Coming to the Table," at CJP's Summer Peacebuilding Institute (SPI). SPI offers courses for credit or for training in 5- to 7-day-long concentrated classes focused on peacebuilding, restorative justice, trauma healing, and other related topics. Both Phoebe and Betty attended, along with 13 others. The group spent three days exploring paths to healing and reconciliation and two days developing ideas for sustaining the CTTT initiative.

PHOEBE: This class was right up my alley. It would show me how I could apply to racial reconciliation all the skills I had learned while getting my Graduate Certificate in Conflict Transformation. I was happy to see Amy spend a lot of time inspiring the group with Psalm 85:10 from the Old Testament—"Truth and Mercy have met together; Peace and Justice have kissed." Earlier in this book, Betty and I have shown how we immediately began using this for our inspiration. We still do today.

The idea of justice was fleshed out with principles drawn from the field of Restorative Justice (RJ). The introductory class I took in RJ focused mostly on Western civil and criminal legal systems and how they apply justice. Someone breaks the law and offends against another. The state legal system sees that the offender is punished for breaking the law. The victim is mostly left out of the process, except to testify in court. RJ was developed to provide a more healing "restorative" alternative to this retributive justice system.

In RJ, the focus is on the victim, or perhaps said more clearly, "the person harmed." As stated by Dr. Howard Zehr in his *Little Book of Restorative Justice*, "Restorative justice requires, at a minimum, that we address the harms and needs of those harmed, hold those causing the harm accountable to 'put right' those harms, and involve both of these parties, as well as relevant communities, in this process." Often, the RJ process involves bringing the victim and offender together, along with interested and affected members of the community, in a conference or circle discussion to answer these questions:

"1. Who has been harmed?
2. What are their needs?
3. Whose obligations are these?

4. Who has a stake in this situation?
5. What are the causes?
6. What is the appropriate process to involve stakeholders in an effort to put things right and address the underlying causes?"
                    —*The Little Book of Restorative Justice*

When I took the class, I saw RJ as applicable mostly to civil or criminal lawbreaking or school disciplinary cases, not bigger picture injustices. Racial oppression in the U.S., starting with slavery and extending to today with all of slavery's legacies, is a lot more complex and far-reaching than a straightforward criminal case or school disciplinary action with one victim and one offender. Slavery is an injustice spread over generations. Many people have been harmed, and many people have done the harming. The whole community, the nation, is involved. It will take a lot to "put things right," to repair the harms.

Initially, I did not see a connection between RJ and what I was doing with Betty. With this Coming to the Table class, and with subsequent research and thought, however, I have come to think differently.

People sometimes ask, "What are we restoring?" If we are honest, we must admit that race relations in the U.S. have rarely been positive, so what are we attempting to restore? The RJ movement has evolved in recent years so that it can offer ways of answering this question. Referring to RJ, Howard Zehr says that "Many advocates see it as a way to restore a sense of hope and community to our world."

Racial and restorative justice advocate Fania Davis has explained her view of RJ in this way: "It's not about returning to the pre-conflict status quo, but about returning to one's best self that's always been there. When well facilitated, RJ processes create the possibility for the transformation of people, relationships, and communities. This is often a radical departure from the pre-conflict status quo. So what are we restoring? For me it's about returning to the part of us that really wants to be connected to one another in a good way. Returning to the goodness inherent in all of us. One might say returning to the divinity present in all of us. Or as indigenous elders put it, returning to that part of us which is related to all things" (*The Little Book of Restorative Justice*).

In the Coming to the Table SPI class, we discussed this information, approaching it intellectually, because, well, we were sitting in a classroom with a teacher and readings and all those cues that tell you that you are in school. But the true breakthroughs started to happen when we began to talk in class about trauma.

CJP offers trainings in "Strategies for Trauma Awareness and Resilience" (STAR). Amy used insights from STAR to talk about the trauma of slavery and racial oppression. According to Amy's instruction, "Trauma is a deep wound that happens when something abnormally shocking, painful, or harmful occurs and leaves us feeling overwhelmed and threatened (physically, emotionally, mentally, or spiritually). This can be a major event or ongoing hurtful experiences."

Depending on the types and level of trauma, and the person, some persons can release the trauma energy. But for some, the trauma symptoms persist, leading to "Post-Traumatic Stress Disorder" or PTSD. Author Joy DeGruy calls this "Post-Traumatic Slave Syndrome," when speaking about the impacts of slavery and its many negative legacies passed down through generations.

Trauma energy that is trapped in the body and brain can lead to a cycle of "acting in" (victimhood) or "acting out" (lashing out to hurt others). Traumatized people can cycle between the two or get stuck in one place as shown in this diagram.

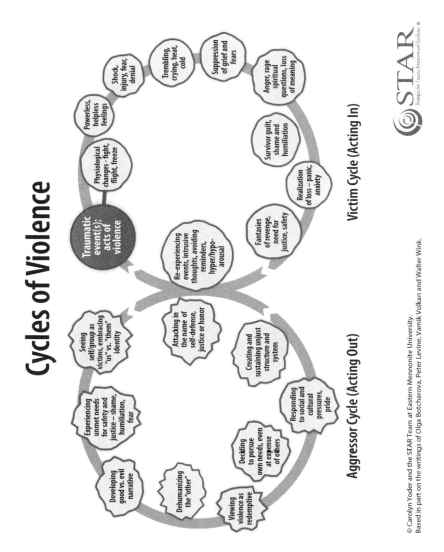

Cycles of Violence Model, Strategies for Trauma Awareness and Resilience Program. Center for Justice and Peacebuilding, Eastern Mennonite University.

One can imagine the power dynamics of slavery that trapped enslavers in the Aggressor Cycle and enslaved persons in the Victim Cycle. Some of these power dynamics cer-

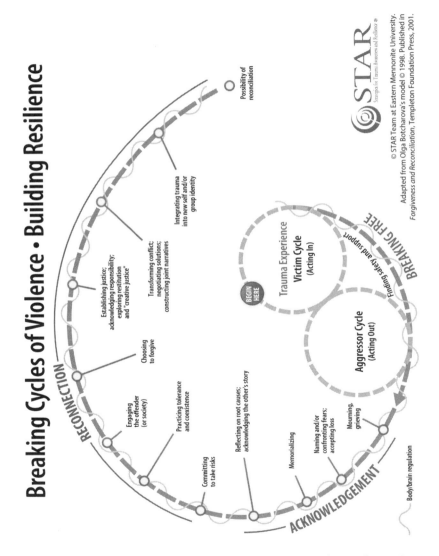

"Snail Model" – Breaking Cycles of Violence - Building Resilience, Strategies for Trauma Awareness and Resilience Program. Center for Justice and Peacebuilding, Eastern Mennonite University.

tainly seem to operate today as people involved in or affected by racial oppression get caught in one cycle or another, or switch back and forth between being a victim or an aggressor.

STAR provides a model for how to break free from this cycle, called the snail model, because of the visual shape of the graphic that describes it. As you can see, it leads to the "possibility of reconciliation," making it an apt model for coming to the table.

To help us visualize and experience the cycles and possibility of breaking free, Amy laid out the models on the classroom floor with rope and words on paper for us to walk around and read in silence and contemplation.

BETTY: I was a pro at burying all my feelings that didn't fit into the picture I had made of myself. I never learned to deal with the trauma of integrating the schools or anything negative or hurtful that came before or after. It was easier for me to bury those feelings and keep moving forward to achieve the goals that I established for myself. No one knew how I felt inside, or what it took for me to walk so tall with my head in the air, looking like I had all the confidence in the world.

I could stand in front of a mirror and confess that I was a child of God, so therefore I had no fear and all fear was gone—but only for a little while. I could tell myself that I can do all things through Christ who strengthens me, and that I was empowered by God's incredible power for that situation. I knew how to pray myself into a place of confidence, power, and control in a crisis situation.

As I walked the circles in class, I was reading words that I knew in my heart were describing me in times throughout my life. I had come to a good place, and I didn't want to remember. But with each step, my covering was falling off.

I was being exposed. I was being forced to look at myself in the mirror in a different light. I didn't want to be that messed up human being. Shock, injury, loss, panic, anger, rage, guilt, shame, humiliation were jumping out, describing me. I kept trying to get outside the circle. I kept telling myself to stay in control. But the more I told myself to stay in control, the weaker I became.

Now I was crying, fearful that I was back in a world of turmoil, fear, and shame, that I was trapped and couldn't find my way out.

I became overwhelmed with emotion. Shay, an African American participant, asked the White people to leave the room. All the African American participants gathered around me and began to pray one after another until I began to gain control of myself. I knew that the individuals who prayed understood what I was going through in my brief moment of insanity. It was hard, and still is, to put into words what happened at that moment when I lost control. When we later joined the rest of the group, we all simply observed a moment of silence.

PHOEBE: Betty's reaction to walking the trauma circles created more understanding among all of us about the impacts of trauma and how difficult it is to break free from its cycles. I am not sure that I can ever truly understand and feel what it has been like for Betty to deal with trauma, but at least this experience gave me some insights.

I contend that a White person can never really understand what it is like to be Black in U.S. society. We can try, but without experiencing it ourselves, I do not think we can truly *know* what it is like. We need to listen to African Americans deeply and take our cues from them about how to best support them and be *our* best selves so we can break free from destructive behaviors.

During the last two days of the SPI class we began to talk about CTTT's future. We brainstormed about what was needed to create and sustain a Coming to the Table movement:

- Coming to the Table should become an "umbrella" organization that nurtures, supports, and extends the work that all CTTT participants are doing for racial reconciliation.
- Ultimately, we hope to become a non-profit organization or be sponsored by or housed within another compatible non-profit organization with similar values and goals.
- After the first gathering in 2006, several participants worked together to draft vision and mission statements and a set of core principles for CTTT. These are a great start, but we need to bring more people to the table to further review and revise these statements before they are adopted.
- In order to make CTTT fundable and sustainable, the group must expand its work beyond just linked descendants to work for racial reconciliation within broader communities and the nation.
- CTTT needs to explore the barriers to racial reconciliation and develop answers to the questions of skeptics. The use of certain words, like "reparations" and "reconciliation" can trigger adverse reactions. We need to consider when to use these words and how to respond to people who react negatively. We may be able to influence moderate sceptics initially. We should focus on them first and hope

to bring more resistant, even initially hostile people, into the fold eventually.

- CTTT needs to address not only slavery, but also its long and continuing legacy of racial oppression and inequity.
- We need an informative website, social media platforms, and programs, trainings, and gatherings in safe spaces that address all interested parties: linked descendants, unlinked descendants, and other Americans.
- CTTT needs to be nonpartisan regarding political party (Democrat, Republican, Libertarian, etc.) and political bent (liberal or conservative).
- We need to partner with other organizations working toward racial reconciliation at the community and national levels.

———◆———

Some additional details were developed, but the list above covers the most sweeping proposals. As I look back on them in 2020, I think that CTTT has accomplished most, if not all, of these goals.

Not too long after the Coming to the Table SPI class, Amy Potter and CJP were able to secure significant funding from the Fetzer Institute and the Kellogg Foundation. Active CTTT participants then began a three-year journey to develop and launch Coming to the Table.

Betty and I joined these volunteers. The grants provided us funds to host a number of retreats—from Kalamazoo, Michigan; to Seattle, Washington; to Tougaloo, Mississippi; to Richmond and Harrisonburg, Virginia. The goal of these retreats was to test theories, principles, and practices that would allow descendants of enslavers and descendants of persons enslaved to work toward reconciliation. Along the way, we shared stories, cried, shouted and railed, hugged, prayed, disagreed, and nodded heads in agreement. We still hug each other today when we meet at CTTT events. That is an achievement in and of itself.

Amy and David Anderson Hooker developed a framework and approach to "transforming historical harms." Originally, we used the word "healing" instead of "transforming." We came to see that it is difficult to achieve complete healing; there will always be some scars. So our goal became "transforming beliefs and structures so that they no longer create circumstances that continue to wound current generations and those to come in the future." This statement appears in the *Transforming Historical Harms Manual*, one of the results of these retreats. It's available on the CTTT website.

In 2019, CTTT Executive Director, Tom DeWolf, and CTTT Board President, Jodie Geddes, took the ideas from this manual and made them more accessible to the public by writing *The Little Book of Racial Healing*, which CTTT now uses as its training manual. In the end, the word "healing" speaks to people. It is certainly something we can aspire to.

In 2012, the major funding ended. CTTT continued as a program under the Center for Justice and Peacebuilding at Eastern Mennonite University for several years, but in 2019, it became a program of Restorative Justice for Oakland Youth (RJOY). You see our website below, along with the Vision and Mission statements. Betty and I were very involved in the development of these and hope they continue to be inspiring and helpful.

www.comingtothetable.org

Vision
Our vision for the United States is of a just
and truthful society that acknowledges
and seeks to heal from the racial wounds
of the past—from slavery and the
many forms of racism it spawned.

Mission
Coming to the Table provides leadership,
resources, and a supportive environment
for all who wish to acknowledge and
heal wounds from racism that is rooted
in the United States' history of slavery.

As we've worked to activate CTTT's vision and mission, we began to use Psalm 85:10 less, and to use instead: "Uncovering History, Making Connections, Working Toward Healing, and Taking Action." These words give people specific things to do. They cover the same territory as the beloved words from the verse—"Truth, Mercy, Justice, and Peace"—but they speak more to logic, to the head, while Psalm 85:10 speaks to the heart. Both are needed.

BETTY: It is always good to gather with a group of like-minded people working together toward a common goal. It allows for talking and working through difficult issues in a safe environment. The glue that holds us together is love for one another.

My children grew up in a diverse school system where they had African American and European American friends. They knew what it felt like to be accepted as part of a diverse group and to feel love and friendship without being on guard all the time. The majority of the time they did not notice their differences or feel discriminated against. I envied them because that was what I wanted.

I have found those feelings among the CTTT group. I didn't have to make sure that my English was always proper out of fear that I would appear to be a second-class citizen. I did have a hard time saying "European Americans" instead of "White people." I had used "White people" for so long, it was unnatural to call my counterparts anything other than "White people." No one ever corrected me or called me out by name for making that mistake.

If I cried, as I usually do, no one asked me why I was crying or tried to talk to me. They simply used love gestures, giving hugs or holding my hand. It has truly become a place for laying down your burdens and experiencing healing.

PHOEBE: When Pat Russell, CTTT's first President, resigned, we all felt that it was important to again have an African American in this post. European Americans have dominated in leadership positions since the country's founding; we wanted to change that pattern. But none of the African Americans on the board volunteered to take the position.

After several requests for volunteers, Betty nominated me. I agreed to take the position until an African American was willing and able. I asserted that I saw myself as a "servant leader" who would use a light touch and serve at the will of the group. I was voted in. I don't remember now if the vote was unanimous, but soon afterwards it became apparent that having me as President just did not sit well with some of the African Americans.

This was still early in my journey of working toward being anti-racist, and I am sure that I said and did things that were considered harming, even racist, by some on the board. As I often say, I grew up in a household and community steeped in racism. I have biases that I try to expunge but I am sure seep out.

Even though many in the group had worked together for several years to birth CTTT, it still was not enough time to instill complete trust. Having a European American as titular leader triggered feelings of resentment among some members of the board. This was manifested in several ways. While board meetings went relatively smoothly in the first year, we soon could not get through our agenda without someone calling people out or strongly objecting to the path we seemed to be following. Mistrust led to calls to make multiple changes to the bylaws to ensure that European Americans would not take over and out-vote the African Americans. This was not happening, but there was concern that it would. We soon elected a board with a majority African American membership.

As CTTT National was forming, people started to meet locally in their own communities. At first, there were only a few local groups. Now there are over 40 CTTT affiliate groups across the U.S. The largest is in Richmond, Virginia, with over 500 members. A few of the local affiliate groups have struggled to develop leadership that is accepted by all. Some have disbanded; a few have reformed.

There have been strong disagreements and rifts, some occurring when I was President of CTTT. While our board has tried at times to heal the rifts, we were not always successful and I feel responsible for some of those failures. After 400 years of slavery and racial oppression, reconciliation is not going to happen quickly or easily. Some doubt that we can ever be reconciled. Some are not sure they want to be reconciled.

BETTY: Change is a very personal and individual commitment, and not everyone was ready for change. But the work is important and must be continued.

PHOEBE: As of 2020, CTTT has had five Board Presidents. I was the only European American.

Go to www.comingtothetable.org to see what CTTT is about today. One accomplishment I would like to highlight is the Reparations Guide posted there.

In December 2014, I hosted a CTTT community conference call on the topic of reparations. The discussion was so lively that we decided to hold another call the next month. Many people joined and offered a variety of ideas about what reparations could look like. We broadened the group further, asking people to email their ideas. Then we set up a Reparations Working Group to review every idea received, which eventually led to the Reparations Guide on the CTTT website. We also researched the activity of other groups working on reparations.

We launched a support campaign for H.R. 40, a resolution sponsored every year since 1989 by U.S. Congressman John Conyers until his death in 2019. It is now sponsored by Rep. Sheila Jackson Lee and proposes a study of reparations by Congress.

Realizing that reparations at the national level will probably take a long time and may never be addressed, we offer in the Guide reparative actions that can be taken at the personal and community level. In 2019, CTTT's Richmond, Virginia, local group made reparations their project for the year. How symbolic and important that this initiative was implemented in the former capital of the Confederacy!

I AM FREE!

BETTY

14

I AM NOW 75 years young. I started this journey when I was 13 because in those times, children were taught to obey their parents. My father ruled our household, so in the beginning, I was just a child obeying my father. As I grew older, I realized that Daddy's way of life had become my way of life because of his strong influence and teaching. The laws in those days forced integration of public schools, and I was just one of those enforcers. Daddy wouldn't let us follow the more militant leaders like Malcom X. In our house we claimed Dr. Martin Luther King, nonviolence, and love for everybody. I learned that you can insist that people follow the law, but you can't mandate people to love each other.

I, too, have a dream. It is to live in a society where we respect one another. I want my children, my grandchildren, and the generations to follow to live in a society where they are not judged by the color of their skin but the content of their character. I dream of a just and peaceful society.

Once during Black History Month, I heard a man tell his story about when he was in second grade in an integrated school in Florida. His White teacher accused him of stealing her lunch in front of the whole class, humiliating this little

Black boy in front of his classmates. The teacher took him to the office where the White principal drilled this little boy to determine the whereabouts of the teacher's lunch. They called the little boy's mother. His mother asked him if he had stolen the teacher's lunch. Through his sobbing and tears, the little boy insisted to his mother that he did not know the whereabouts of the teacher's lunch.

Just as the White principal was about to hand down the little boy's punishment, the teacher walked into the principal's office and announced that she had found her lunch. The little boy was sent back to his class with all his classmates thinking he was a thief. The damage was done. No one apologized to the little boy in public or in private. What do you think the other students learned from this event?

The young man was 26 years old when I heard him tell his story. This had happened 20 years earlier. I still felt his pain as he told his story. I cringed because once upon a time I owned his pain, and I took on the guilt for every child that suffered at the hands of mean-spirited White people in integrated schools.

I talked with a Native American woman who informed me that when she was a little girl, she went to an integrated school. The teacher put her desk in the coat room. What do you think her classmates learned from this event? She cried as she told me her story. I could feel her pain.

I spoke with a White man who told me that as a little boy he was bused to an African American elementary school. He said the little Black boys beat him up every day and took his lunch money.

I reached out and hugged him and apologized for what he had to endure. He didn't reject me or blame me for what the little Black boys did to him. His family moved in order to get him out of that traumatic situation.

Lots of people tell me their stories. It's a good opportunity for them to be able to tell somebody who understands. Each time it breaks my heart.

I sold many of my books on military bases where there is a lot of diversity within families. People brought their mixed children to me and asked if I had advice to help them navigate a racist society. As I looked at the faces of those beautiful little brown and almost-White children, I thought about my very own children, grandchildren, and great-grandchildren. I told the parents to teach their children to love everybody and above all to love themselves. I said that I looked at myself in the mirror in the mornings before I left for school, and I reminded myself that I was a child of God, full of grace and beauty. I loved myself because God made me, and God doesn't make no junk.

I attended my husband David's high school class reunion. He graduated from an all-Black high school in 1964. He played sports and was a football hero during those days. The students talked about their Black teachers who took their students' learning and preparation for the real world seriously. If they had plans for college, one teacher in particular made sure they had the appropriate classes for college success. If they weren't planning on college, he made sure they had a trade and that they would to be able to get a job after high school.

African American students who attended high school in the Colored school system believe that integration was not a good thing, because with integration, they lost the love and caring of their Colored/Black/African American teachers. This was an undeniable fact because many African American teachers lost their jobs, and many African American schools sat empty and lifeless for years. I believe that I shared blame for this, too.

During my college days I was introduced to Willie Lynch. Lynch was purportedly a British slave owner in the West Indies.

The story is that he was invited to the colony of Virginia in 1712 to teach his methods of breaking slaves to slave owners in Virginia. His methods were brutal. Even though this man and his speech are now considered by some historians to be a hoax, I was deeply affected by what I was told and read. It helped me to understand my own family. It became a wedge that started to open my mind so I could eventually refuse to allow differences to block friendships and instead accept others who I once couldn't.

Lynch taught slave owners to break their female slaves as they would a horse. He believed that having experienced this, female slaves would train their children in the same way. How does one ever escape this? I thought about the rape I experienced in high school. I was a broken spirit for a long time after it. Yes, it kept me quiet for many years. However, when I began to write about the experience, I lifted it out of my soul, my body, and my spirit, and I began to be freed. I no longer lived in fear that the boys—now men—would come back to destroy me. In fact, I was willing to die rather than live in fear. Not only was I free from my past, I could now see how this other brutality and fear affected my ancestors, even my very own father. Not only did it have a merciless impact on people of color, it deeply affected European Americans negatively.

Getting an education was the best thing that could have happened to me. Not only did I learn and grow, it allowed me to take back what the devil stole from me. Many of the classes that I took at Lord Fairfax Community College gave me back my self-esteem and self-worth.

When I realized that I had the ability to learn and make good grades, I knew there was something wrong with many things that I assumed about myself. I had accepted as facts what some individuals in White society—teachers and others of influence—had said, intentionally meaning to hurt me and keep me in a state of low self-esteem. So when I graduated from Lord Fairfax Community College, I applied for the Business and Professional Women's Scholarship, and I won it.

This was the early 1980s, and a turning point in my life. The scholarship was a real boost. It was not about the money, because Rubbermaid was paying for my education through its tuition reimbursement program. But the very fact that I could learn and accomplish something let me know that the past was wrong. I had experienced trauma. Now I was breaking through the trauma.

I began to realize that I was not responsible for what every African American child endured during integration. I was not responsible for what every Native American child endured during integration. I was not responsible for what every European American endured during integration. I was not responsible for the journey of my ancestors. I was not responsible for my daddy losing his land. I am, however, responsible for the decisions that I make, my actions and responses to situations. I am responsible to seek the truth and acknowledge my history, and I must share this knowledge with the next generation.

Nearly 25 years later, in 2007, Phoebe, a European American woman contacts me. I thank God she waited until I was ready to take this journey with her. I had needed time—years—in order to be able to reply genuinely, "Hello, Cousin."

Our friendship has evolved into kinship. Phoebe and I went together to Oakland, California, in June of 2017 to present at the National Association of Community and Restorative Justice conference (NACRJ). We stayed with Phoebe's sister Margaret. We hung out and had a great time, laughing, talking, and having fun. We were family.

The next day, Phoebe and I were to make our presentation with Jodie Geddes from Coming to the Table. I was like that little duck who's all calm above water, but whose feet are moving like crazy under the water. That was me. I believe I cried through the entire presentation.

Dr. Joy DeGruy developed the theory of Post Traumatic Slave Syndrome (PTSS). According to Dr. DeGruy, "It is a condition that exists as a consequence of multigenerational oppression of Africans and their descendants resulting from centuries of chattel slavery. A form of slavery which was predicated on the belief that African Americans were inherently/ genetically inferior to Whites. This was then followed by institutionalized racism which continues to perpetuate injury."

This is me. I seem to experience these PTSS emotional breakdowns at the most inopportune times. Understanding that I am not super-human allows me to forgive myself and keep moving forward. I have PTSS and I can deal with that.

Getting to know ancestors' stories from both sides of our Kilby African American and European American family has also contributed to my growing self-esteem and healing.

In 2010, I was at Disney World in Florida when I received a call from Dr. Tracy Fitzsimmons of Shenandoah University in Winchester, Virginia. She asked me to speak at the summer graduation in August and to receive an Honorary Degree, Doctor of Humane Letters.

Betty receives an Honorary Doctoral Degree, Shenandoah University.

Daddy had always wanted a doctor in the family. But I had let go of the dream of getting a doctoral degree when I was given custody of my grandchildren. Now here was an opportunity.

Honorary Degree
Citation

BETTY KILBY FISHER BALDWIN
Doctor of Humane Letters

Few people in our world have had the opportunity to participate in the beginning and the unfinished promise of an important historical moment. Betty Kilby Fisher Baldwin has. In the 1950s Virginia faced the civil rights movement as an antagonist with its Massive Resistance laws that closed public schools rather than integrate them. In *Betty Ann Kilby vs. The Warren County Board of Education,* civil rights leaders invoked her name on behalf of all children in Virginia to challenge school segregation and won.

In her autobiography *Wit, Wills and Walls* Betty Kilby Fisher Baldwin not only contributes to the details of the history of the civil rights movement and provides hope for the future of race relations in American society, she also warns us how easily a principle can slip away without constant conscious attention.

For her role in the civil rights movement, her translation of the principle of equality for all people into very human terms, as a life-long interpreter and *advocate extraordinaire,* and a daughter of this institution, Shenandoah University is honored to award Betty Kilby Fisher Baldwin the degree, Doctor of Humane Letters, *honoris causa.*

Presented Saturday, August 14, 2010
Shenandoah University, Winchester, Virginia

It was not an asset that would push me up a corporate ladder, but I was still excited.

At the graduation, I told the students how I had come to the college 16 years after graduating from high school. My high school years were traumatic. My grades were unacceptable. I was not college material. But I did not let that stop me from pursuing my dream. I advised the students to never give up on their dreams and to reach beyond average.

I felt free. I had achieved Daddy's dream of having a doctor in the family, but more personally, I had not allowed anyone to steal my dream. Despite all the obstacles, I got my formal education, plus now an honorary Doctor of Humane Letters. No one can take any of that from me.

COMPLICITY IN THE OPPRESSION 15

PHOEBE

SOME SAY, "SLAVERY was so long ago. You were not responsible for your family's enslaving. Just let this go." But as I think about my family and the racism I witnessed within them and within myself, I recognize that uncovering our involvement with slavery was just the beginning of what I was to discover. Soon after finishing my research on my family's participation in slavery, I decided that I needed to uncover and face up to whatever else my family did regarding the oppression of Black people since the end of the Civil War up to today. And that included my own complicity in this oppression.

The story of oppressing African Americans did not stop with slavery. A short period of Reconstruction followed the Civil War. Emancipated slaves were given some new opportunities, although not their 40 acres and a mule. And a number of them surged ahead to become leaders. But this was soon followed by the period of Redemption, described in detail by Henry Louis Gates, Jr., in his 2019 book, *Stony the Road*.

During this time, many European Americans, particularly Southerners, began to re-write history—describing the Civil War as a fight for Southern rights, instead of being about slavery, and creating myths that masters were good to their slaves and that the slaves and their progeny were intellectually deficient, incompetent, and incapable of taking care of themselves. This led to the Jim Crow years, when the rights of African Americans were seriously infringed upon, their access to education was limited, and many were terrorized through mass incarceration, prison labor camps, and lynching.

I have not discovered any narratives that describe how African Americans fared in Rappahannock County immediately after Emancipation. That is research for another book. Lillian Freeman Aylor, an African American who was born in 1938, writes in her 2019 book, *I'll Get it Done: A Life Journey in Rappahannock County*, about knowing of Ku Klux Klan members living in the county during her lifetime. Old folks used to talk to her about a lynching in Huntly, Virginia, an unincorporated area in Rappahannock County. Interactions between Black men and White women often resulted in the men leaving the county for fear of lynching. Lillian laments that even today White people ride around the county with Confederate flags flying from their cars and pickups.

She also describes a county when she was growing up where education for Black children was provided in separate schools and only through the seventh grade. Like the Kilby children, Black children who wanted to attend high school had to go the "Manassas Industrial Institute," a boarding school in Manassas, Virginia, or be bused to another high school for Black children in a neighboring county, in this case Washington Carver Regional High School in Culpeper County. Deseg-regation in Rappahannock County did not occur until 1966.

After learning about Betty's and James's struggles with integrating Warren County Schools, I wanted to know if any of my family had participated in the implementation of seg-regated schools in Rappahannock County. I spent a day in the county's school board offices reading minutes of the board. I found that my grandfather, Walter Bluford Kilby, known as "Watt," served on the board from 1922 to 1929, when the county's schools were segregated. The minutes showed that the board took the following actions to provide and enforce segregated schools:

- On January 1, 1923, the board votes "to build a Colored school building at Washington… in the coming summer."
- On October 1, 1923, they approve contracts for providing wood for the heating of White and Colored schools.
- On October 19, 1925, the board held a special meeting to hear a petition from A.S. Bowersett in which he asks that Helen Coghill and Major Coghill be excluded from attending one of the White schools. "… he has been informed that said children are not White." The board then instructs the school's teacher, Mrs. Margaret Rucker Bowersett, to exclude the children.
- On October 4, 1926, the board discusses hiring a "Colored teacher" for one of the Colored schools, and again buying wood for heating of the White and Colored schools.

The minutes continue to show various actions taken by the board to administer segregated schools throughout my grand-father's tenure. My grandfather was part of the Jim Crow sys-tem.

Did other members of my family support educational inequality in Rappahannock County? I found answers when I reviewed school board minutes from the 1950s and '60s. In the minutes for July 21, 1954, I found the school board discussing the Brown vs. Board of Education decision and the opinion issued by J. Lindsay Almond, then the Virginia Attorney General, authorizing local school boards to "proceed on the same organizational basis for the 1954-55 session as had been done in previous years." In other words, ignore the U.S. Supreme Court. This policy was in force when my uncle, my father's brother, joined the school board in September, 1956.

Segregated schools continued while my uncle was on the board until 1966. That September, forced by the Civil Rights Act of 1964, the Rappahannock County schools opened as integrated schools, six and one-half years after Betty and James walked up that hill to integrate Warren County High School.

An interesting entry in the school board minutes is found for the meeting of October 14, 1958, when my uncle was chairman of the board and just after Governor J. Lindsay Almond had closed Warren County High School as part of Massive Resistance: "The Superintendent presented a request from a number of Warren County parents for permission to enroll their children in the Rappahannock County High School, Washington, Virginia. Some of the children have moved into Rappahannock County and are living there with relatives. Others wish to commute daily from Warren County to Washington, Virginia. After a full discussion of this meeting, the Board expressed the feeling that it was the desire of said Board to cooperate as completely as possible with the Warren County parents for permission to enroll their children in the Rappahannock County High School, Washington, Virginia." The motion to admit these students was unanimously approved.

In 1958, the Rappahannock County Schools were still segregated, and Rappahannock County High School was for Whites only. My uncle and Rappahannock County were helping the White parents from neighboring Warren County, as Betty and James were scrambling to find a place to go to school while the Virginia Supreme Court considered their case. This was complicity in Massive Resistance.

I have found no evidence that my grandparents engaged in sharecropping as was occurring on the Finks farm, when Betty's grandparents and father worked for Old Man Dick Finks down the road. My grandparents had children to do the work on their farm and occasionally hired a White woman to live with them and help, as shown in the U.S. Census. They and their children prospered enough that my father's older sisters went to college and became teachers. Then they were able to help my father pay his tuition to attend the University of Virginia for his bachelor's and medical degrees.

My father undoubtedly developed his racial attitudes from his parents, who developed them from their parents, the attitudes continuing back to our first ancestor on this continent, John Kilby, who was an enslaver in the early 1700s. I speculate that enslaving requires one to disregard the humanity of those that you enslave, and that this inevitably creates prejudices in the mind to justify your actions. These prejudices are passed down.

I never met my grandfather Watt Kilby, since he died before I was born, but I have told you about my grandmother, whose family also included enslavers. She was affronted by Inez, who my parents employed as a maid, because Inez dared to come to the front door to enter our house.

In a conversation I had with a cousin who grew up in Rappahannock County, he told me that our grandmother resented that there were Black folks in the county who "used" the name Kilby. My father picked up these attitudes because he was surrounded by them, not just in Rappahannock County, but most places he went. One of those places was the University of Virginia.

In November 2013, Betty and I were asked to speak at a conference at the University of Virginia, entitled "Virginia Universities and their Race Histories." It was fascinating to hear various speakers from the University of Virginia, the College of William & Mary, Washington & Lee University, Hampden-Sydney College, and others speak about their universities' connections to slavery, Jim Crow, and later oppressions of African Americans.

I remember listening intently to a presentation about the UVA Medical School being a center for the study of the pseudo-science eugenics in the 1920s and '30s. According to the March 2014 edition of *The Virginia Advocate*, the student magazine of the University of Virginia, "(T)he goal of eugenics was to help 'improve' the genetic element of the human population. The movement's greatest proponents encouraged reproduction between people who had desirable traits and discouraged reproduction with anyone with less desirable traits. Conspicuously, eugenicists often linked these traits to race and ethnicity."

Dr. Harvey E. Jordan, a professor in the medical school, was a proponent of eugenics, "and he even lobbied for forced sterilization to prevent human beings from reproducing if they had traits that were deemed less desirable. Between 1927 and 1979 about 8,300 such 'undesirable' Virginians underwent forced sterilization." Furthermore, "At the height of the eugenics movement, this social science had further advanced the idea of White racial superiority and anti-Semitism at the University of Virginia and in the Southern aristocratic families at large."

As I sat listening to this talk, I was calculating when my father attended medical school at UVA. I thought it was some time in the 1930s. I knew that I had a large photo of his graduating class at home. When I found it, the story was all there. The photo included cameo portraits of all the students and professors. Right below my father's portrait was that of

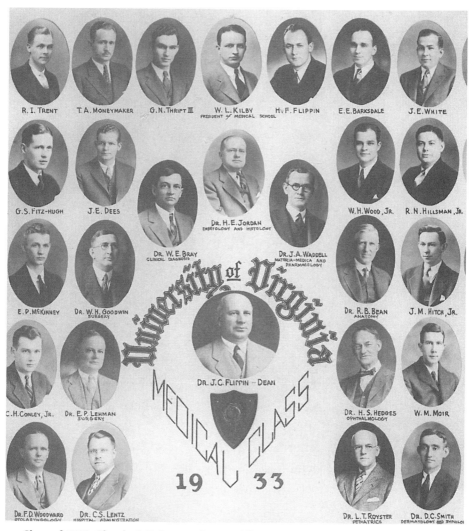

Class of 1933. Phoebe's father, Walter L. Kilby, at center top; Dr. H.E. Jordan immediately below.

Dr. H.E. Jordan. My father must have studied eugenics. Any prejudices he already had were reinforced by the "science" taught him in medical school.

This was quite the revelation, because I had never heard my father speak about eugenics, although everything he said about "Negros" was disparaging. But as I thought about it more, I began to see my father in a different light. He, like all of us, was a product of his time and place. Here was his medical school teaching him that Negros were genetically inferior. No wonder he had the attitudes he did.

I was a science major, with degrees in Botany and Environmental Management. My sister also majored in science. I called to tell her about my discovery. I asked her, "Margaret, when we were at Duke, did we believe that our professors were telling us the truth?"

"Yes."

"This was science. It was based on careful research and a desire to uncover the facts, right?"

"Yes."

"So, can we blame our dad for believing that what he was being taught in medical school was the truth?"

We both agreed that we could not. I had not questioned my professors, and neither had he, it appeared.

My father ended up practicing medicine in Baltimore, Maryland, a city with deep racial divisions. He and my mother purchased a home in Guilford, a neighborhood where all the lots had covenants written into the deeds that you could not sell to a Negro. Baltimore was famous for this and its redlining. Indeed, my neighborhood was completely "White," and so were the neighborhoods of all my friends.

When I was very young, my mother redecorated the waiting room in my father's medical office downtown. I accompanied her when she went to the office as she took measurements, chose fabrics at the upholsterer's shop, and selected pictures for the walls and lamps and knickknacks for the tables. She spent a while measuring the waiting room, so I wandered down the hall and opened another door. I found a small, bare, windowless room with a few hard, wooden chairs, the "Colored waiting room." I was learning that White people got the nice comfy chairs in the pretty sunlit room.

I quickly picked up my father's attitudes. My mother told me later in life that once at age four, I called Inez the N-word. I don't remember doing that, but I do remember that Inez never liked me very much. She liked my sister Margaret much better, bringing her little presents when she came to work.

My friends and I watched TV shows like "Amos & Andy," and we loved to joke around using the King Fish's dialect. When I was a teenager, my favorite movie was "Gone with the Wind." It was so romantic, and I laughed with everyone else in the theater when Mammy talked: "It ain't fittin'. It jes' ain't fittin'.'" We swam at the Meadowbrook Swim Club, which I have found through later research was a private club that excluded "Negros," because most of the City pools were integrated.

When I was ready to go to school, my parents sent me to Bryn Mawr, a private girl's school (Pre-K through 12th grade), established in 1885 as the first college-preparatory school for girls in the United States. That sounds pretty cool, a school for feisty girls established by feisty women. But Bryn Mawr was for Whites only. I speculate that when I was ready to start school in 1956, my parents sent me there, at least in part, because the Baltimore City Schools had integrated in 1954.

My class did not integrate until 1967, when we were sophomores in high school. Two girls, Darlene and Marsha, joined us. I did not share many classes with them, but I did share homeroom. Our homeroom in our senior year was like a big living room with couches and big chairs and a record player with speakers. We all loved "Soul Music"—the Temptations, the Supremes, Marvin Gaye, Ike and Tina Turner, Stevie Wonder. And we loved to dance to our favorite songs. I remember that we would beg Darlene to show us how to dance. (Darlene was the outgoing one; Marsha was kind of shy.) Darlene always refused. "Oh, come on, Darlene, show us how to dance!!" We assumed she had rhythm and was a good dancer. I cringe now when I think of this. Was Marsha hurt because we did not ask her, or relieved?

In the documentary film of Betty's book, *Wit, Will & Walls*, one of the commentators notes that none of Betty's White classmates ever befriended her. When I think back to Bryn Mawr, I realize that I never made an effort to reach out to Darlene or Marsha. I was shy and also a victim of bullying with not much social self-confidence, but that is really no excuse. I could have done more.

The editors of our graduating class yearbook seemed to have somewhat of a free hand with its content. What I remember most was our very casual class photo. I am sitting on the ground in the front with my knee up in a kind of cheesecake pose. But, hey, look at Darlene standing in the back row, third from the left. I couldn't believe it when I first saw this photo. I knew exactly what she was doing with her fist in the air. That was a Black power fist from the 1968 Summer Olympics. I never talked to Darlene about her thoughts on race, but this fist said everything. I did not know how to talk to Darlene. I had grown up in such a White world that I did not know how to relate to African Americans. I was afraid of saying the wrong thing. I think I was afraid that she would tell me how racist I was.

Class of 1970, The Bryn Mawr School, Baltimore, Maryland. Phoebe shown in the front row, seated. Darlene Pledger shown in the back row.

1968 Olympics Black Power fist.

I wish I could apologize for all the things I did or did not do that harmed Darlene and Marsha. So far, I have been unsuccessful at contacting Darlene. As this book goes to press, I have been able to connect with Marsha. We had a pleasant phone conversation, but one conversation is not enough to explore the Bryn Mawr experience in full. I hope to connect with her further.

I can say that by high school, I had already begun to pull away from my family's racist views. Thank goodness for my American history teacher, Mrs. McDaniel. In my senior year, she offered an unusual class. If we read our American history textbook during the summer and passed a test at the beginning of the year, we could join this class and study trends in history that related to current issues. One segment was on the history of African Americans and the Civil Rights movement. We were assigned to read *Black Like Me* by John Howard Griffin. That was, and still is, one of the most terrifying books I have ever read. In the 1950s, Griffin, a White man, went through a process of darkening his skin to appear Black, and then traveled through the southern U.S. He was demeaned and terrorized during the entire journey. Also during this period, I read the *Autobiography of Malcom X* and *Soul on Ice* by Eldridge Cleaver. This was the beginning of my education about the injustices and oppression of African Americans.

Later, when I took an introductory sociology class in college, I wrote a paper on the image and treatment of African Americans in children's books found in the college library. I went through the entire collection, pulling every 10th book and reporting on what I found. Most of the children and parents pictured in the books were White, except for some Negro children in fairy tales like "Little Black Sambo." There was a book about jobs you could have when you grew up. The professionals, like doctors, were White (and male). I'll never forget one book that was about "the city." The people were all White, until you got to the page about "the ghetto." There was a Black family walking down the street barefooted, in tattered overalls and print dresses, with the father wearing a straw hat. It was a ridiculous image. What children were learning from their books was tainted with bias and untruths. These were the kinds of books I read as a child.

I did not pursue sociology as a major, instead getting degrees that led me to a career in environmental planning. My first job was with the city of Durham, North Carolina, in 1976. I had attended Duke University, which is located in Durham, and most of the students were White. Only when I started working for the city government did I meet and get to know African Americans in the city. Durham was about 40% Black at that time, and the City Planning Department had a number of Black employees, including Dwight Yarborough and Wayne Smith. The Planning Director, Dexter Smith, was White.

I have to thank Dwight and Wayne for educating me about the state of Black Durham. Dwight pointed out to me that the neighborhood he had grown up in, Hayti, was divided and destroyed by the construction of the Durham Freeway. State and Federal transportation departments often located urban freeways through Black neighborhoods, because those neighborhoods were designated "blighted," and the residents had little power.

Wayne Smith made me laugh, because he loved to go up to the Planning Director, Dexter Smith, put his arm around him, and introduce him as his cousin. He would get this big grin on this face, while Dexter looked stricken and squirmed out of the hug. I never thought that they could be cousins, and I don't think Wayne did either. Smith is a common name. But who knows, maybe they are cousins, just like Betty and me.

When a White non-profit proposed a program to City Council to help Black children, the African American members of the Council objected, saying that such a program should be run by African Americans. The proposal was voted down. I was somewhat baffled by this, because these White people were trying to do something good. But I was also beginning to see that Black empowerment was just as important.

After I left Durham, I worked for Fairfax County, Virginia, and then became a planning consultant. I wrote environmental impact statements and prepared long-range plans for cities, counties, parks, and historic sites. When I was asked to serve on the Shenandoah Valley Battlefields National Historic District Commission, I was excited about the opportunity. Our group consulted with historians and planners to develop an initial plan for preserving the Civil War battlefields of the Shenandoah Valley in Virginia. I saw this as an opportunity to preserve farmland and open space. We made sure that the plan emphasized that interpretation of the history should include unbiased portrayals of the actions and perspectives of both Union and Confederate forces.

The history of the people of the Valley was also to be told, but I bought what the historians told us—that there was not much to say about slavery, because Valley farmers had few slaves. In 2019, when Betty and I were asked to make a presentation at a conference sponsored by the Shenandoah Valley Battlefields Foundation, we learned from the other speakers that this was not true. There was plenty to tell.

I worked quite a bit with historians and architectural historians during my career, repeating their principles—one could say mantras—on historic preservation. These emphasized the preservation, restoration, and rehabilitation of historic properties, but never reconstruction of what had been lost to destruction and decay. That was not preserving history, it was creating it, some calling it the "Disneyfication of history."

In 2013, six years after I began participating in Coming to the Table, I attended a conference at Monticello called "Telling the History of Slavery." One of the last sessions involved speakers and a panel discussion about whether slave dwellings should be reconstructed at historic sites like Monticello. As I listened to one speaker repeat the mantra of "no reconstruction," it dawned on me that this was just another excuse, based on "principle," to hide the true history of African Americans. Slavery dwellings were by their very nature ephemeral. They were not built to last like "the big house." All the slave dwellings on Monticello's Mulberry Row were long gone. If you did not reconstruct these dwellings, one could argue that you were hiding Thomas Jefferson's practice of enslavement. No one in the audience was challenging this historian. I decided I had to speak up and did so.

The lead historian at Monticello came to me afterwards and said that the caretakers of the site were already on their way to changing their policy of no reconstruction. A reconstructed slave dwelling has now been built and is open for visitors at Monticello today.

For a long time, I was complicit in hiding slave dwellings and the history of slavery at historic sites. Coming to the Table has helped me recognize my complicity and work to do something about it.

TOGETHER ON THE ROAD 16

BETTY AND PHOEBE

PHOEBE: AFTER BETTY and I first met in February, 2007, she returned to her home in Texas, and I remained in Virginia. We both wanted to get to know each other better, but doing that by phone was just not satisfying. Then other opportunities arose. Amy Potter at the Center for Justice and Peacebuilding, who had organized the first Coming to the Table gathering in 2006, began applying to various organizations, asking to give presentations about CTTT at their conferences. Amy had been present at Betty's and my first meeting at the theater where the film "Wit, Will & Walls" was premiered, and I was a colleague of hers at EMU. She asked us to join her at these conferences as living examples of people "coming to the table."

Betty and I jumped at the chance to join Amy; we saw it as a way to learn to know each other. We would stay at hotels and eat meals together.

Amy did most of the presenting early on since we did not yet have much lived experience together to recount. But people in the audience were intrigued by what Betty and I were attempting together. They told their own stories, and we learned a lot from them. Increasingly, we shaped these events as sharing sessions, where everyone learned about each other's family histories, struggles with racism, and hopes and dreams for a better world.

The first conference that Betty and I attended with Amy was the Gandhi-King Conference on Peacemaking in Memphis, Tennessee. We had our first deep moment of sharing there. And then it happened again and again—at the National Conference on Dialogue and Deliberation in Austin, Texas; at The Anatomy of Reconciliation, Restorative Justice, and Healing Conference in Tuskegee, Alabama; and at the White Privilege Conference in La Crosse, Wisconsin. Soon people and organizations started asking Betty and me directly to come and speak. By then we had had many "coming to the table" experiences together, including the Coming to the Table Summer Peacebuilding Institute class and all those activities with Betty's brother James Kilby to commemorate the integration of Warren County High School. One of those experiences set the stage for future presentations.

When James and I were working on the school integration commemoration, we met often at a little diner in Front Royal for lunch and strategy sessions. James is a Baptist minister, so he would say the blessing for our meal. I will never forget that first time when he started speaking. He said word for word the exact same grace that my father used to say every night at the dinner table. We had a common grace! Soon after this, Betty and I started entitling our presentations, "A Common Grace."

BETTY: I remember one time when Phoebe picked me up at the airport. We spent the night in a nice hotel. We had dinner together. My prayer for the meal was not the same as my brother James's. Phoebe was surprised. Our vision of our presentation, "A Common Grace," was different.

I explained that my vision for our "Common Grace" was that God has given us both grace to forgive the past. We can't be effective until we have the grace to forgive and replace hate and all our emotional hurt with love.

The more we spoke about a common grace with our audiences, the more we began to see that we were inviting all of the people there to join us at the table and share a common grace.

PHOEBE: Betty is a good teacher. I think that many people who attended our presentations came to understand Betty's interpretation of "A Common Grace."

From 2007 to early 2020, Betty and I made about 25 presentations together. But it was that first one at the Gandhi-King Conference on Peacemaking in Memphis, Tennessee, that impacted us the most personally.

BETTY: It had been a little over 15 years since I had lived and worked in Memphis. I arrived in Memphis for the conference carrying both emotional and physical baggage. I was living in Cleburne, Texas, recently divorced after 43 years of marriage, and I was raising two grandchildren. It had been a while since the last time I had presented my story, and this would be the first I was sharing the presentation with a group. To say that I was balled into knots would have been an understatement.

I had a good drive from Cleburne to Memphis. Driving was always a good time for me to relax, reflect, and get my emotions in shape. If it was a crying time, I would cry until I had no tears left to cry. That way no one would realize how truly vulnerable I was.

I was excited to be a part of something as significant as a Gandhi-King Conference on Peacemaking. The fact that it was in Memphis, Tennessee, conjured up my memories of working at Northwest Airlink, where I was fired for the first time in my career. My boss wanted me to do some things outside the scope of my job, and I refused. I wanted to quit, but quitting would have been the same as failing. Besides, I could not allow a White man to intimidate me without fighting back.

Whenever I needed a cup of courage during that time, I would go to the National Civil Rights Museum at the Lorraine Motel during my lunch break and sit outside. Just thinking about Dr. King's sacrifice and his journey inspired me to keep on fighting injustice.

PHOEBE: At the time of the conference in Memphis, I was still in the early stages of researching my family's connections to slavery and to Betty's family. One evening as we sat in our shared hotel room in our pajamas, I laid out copies of all the historical documents I had collected so far about my family and Betty's. I showed her the 1865 court case when my great-grandfather's cousin, Mortimer Kilby, was suing his mother Malinda for the ownership of five slaves—Juliet and her four children, Simon, John, James, and Sarah. I already suspected that Simon was Betty's great-grandfather, but I wasn't completely sure. I had found evidence of Simon living in Rappahannock County, Virginia, where my ancestors lived after the end of the Civil War, including a marriage license for him and his bride Lucy Frances Wallace. Accompanying the license was a handwritten note that I also showed to Betty:

"F.T Meeting House, RappH County, Va Dec 29th, 1873

Col. R.M. Heterick

Dear Sir,
This will be handed you by Simon Kilby (Colored)
who waits on you for license, His Father & Mother
are both dead, He has been raised immediately in my
neighborhood, his age is not known to the day. But
I will say to you that he is over Twenty-One years
of age. You will find enclosed a Certificate of Mrs.
Martha Wallace (Colrd) which was signed in my
presence Which fact I certify to you. The father of the
young lady is not known. You will please issue license
to the parties & I will [undecipherable] you all right.

Truly Yr. Friend,
P.M. Finks"

Because the handwriting was hard to read, Betty took some
time to read the note. When she put the paper down, she hung
her head and cried. I had not expected that this would make
her cry.

BETTY: Sometimes, no matter how much I cried in an appropriate place, I could still not control my emotions. Having
dealt with the White man's thumb one time already that day,
here we were again. Phoebe was trying with all her might to
figure out the connection between our families. I know how
hard and time-consuming this research is because I researched
Warren County's history for a school project.

The very reason we shared a hotel room during our journey together was so we could know and understand each other better. It was difficult on both sides. It was complicated. This was "coming to the table" in action.

Perplexed, Phoebe asked, "Are you okay?" I answered, "Just when you think you have the past wrapped up in a neat little package, it comes back to haunt you. No matter how bad it hurts, we must continue to discuss slavery and its impact."

I was wondering if Mortimer was the father of Juliet's children. I concluded that Mortimer sued his mother for Juliet and her four children because this was also his family. Right or wrong, this is the story I chose to believe. That document was dated 1865; it was so close to the end of slavery. What did it matter? Was Juliet my ancestor?

The second document that Phoebe handed me was dated December 29, 1873. I saw P.M. Finks' signature and I couldn't think. It was like waving a red flag in front of a bull. Growing up, I heard stories of Old Man Dick Finks and how he controlled and terrorized my grandparents and father. I opened my book to see if this note writer was Old Man Dick Finks from the stories I heard as a child. The P.M (Dick) Finks from my childhood was born October 7, 1889. So, this was his grandfather, placing his thumb on my great-grandparents Simon and Lucy Frances. They could not marry without his consent!

Phoebe had read the stories about Old Man Dick Finks in my book, and she probably understood that I would not allow myself to be drawn into the past. No, not the night before the conference. It was still much too upsetting. We can't change the past. All we can do is learn from it and make sure the mistakes of the past aren't repeated. I closed my eyes and dreamed that one day Phoebe and I would show the world

how we took on the issues of race and reconciliation one step
and one day at a time.

PHOEBE: Why hadn't I foreseen that this might upset Betty?
I wanted to hug her, to help her feel better and know that
someone cared. Yet I was descended from oppressors. My family probably knew the Finks. (I would later discover that they
went to church together.) Would she really want someone like
me hugging her? I cannot remember now whether I hugged
her. But as I learned over time, the trauma of White oppression
of her great-grandparents, grandparents, and father was at the
hands of the Finks family in her view. She never seemed to
show resentment toward the White Kilbys. I guess that is one
reason that she could be open to meeting me. But even then, I
had no illusions that my family had been kind to Betty's great-
great-grandmother Juliet or Juliet's mother, Sarah.

Going to conferences together was very much a part of our
own "coming to the table" and over time offered opportunities
for others to begin their "coming to the table "experiences.

I remember an older White woman standing up after one
presentation with tears in her eyes. She found it difficult to
speak, but was finally able to tell us that the presentation had
prompted memories of her childhood. When she visited her
grandparents, she and her siblings and cousins liked to go up
to the attic to play with the old toys and artifacts up there.
Listening to us, she realized that some of those artifacts were
chains with manacles, chains once used on enslaved persons.
No one chastised her for this revelation. We understood her
grief.

Then there was the time, years after my genealogical research visit with Aunt Lucia, that Betty and I made a presentation at the retirement community where Aunt Lucia then lived. I was not sure what she would make of my journey with Betty. But after we showed Betty's film and talked about our connections, Aunt Lucia stood up and told the crowd that she was my aunt and that she was very glad to meet Betty. Afterwards, she came up to Betty to shake her hand. Her big smile told me that she meant it.

Phoebe's Aunt Lucia.

BETTY: My favorite presenting venues were the ones where family was able to come and just be there in the audience to support us. My children, grandchildren, my brother James, his wife Janice, his daughter Racquelia, Phoebe's sister Margaret and cousin Tim, my sister-in-law Peggy, and so many other family members came to our presentations. It was an added benefit when we could fellowship afterwards.

On a Sunday afternoon in March of 2008, Phoebe and I did a presentation at Busboys and Poets Café in Washington D.C. The place has a large room with a stage for its weekly poetry night and book signings. They have "cuisine for the body, curated events for the mind, and powerful poetry for the soul."

Phoebe stayed with her sister Margaret, and they came to the presentation together. I came to the city early in order to spend some time with family in the area. I stayed with my daughter Renee and her family. My son-in-law Charles was working at Howard University as Dean of Student Affairs, and he was able to get me an interview with Triscina Gray on Howard University's Radio WHUR to advertise the Busboys and Poets event.

Renee and Bettina both lived in the Washington D.C. metropolitan area. Between Bettina's friends, Renee's friends, Phoebe's family and friends, the WHUR interview, and Busboys and Poets' advertising, we packed the house. We spoke and showed my film, "Wit, Will & Walls."

When we asked the audience to share their stories with us, there was a brief silence. Then Bettina and Renee got up to introduce themselves. The microphone was handed to Bettina. "Hello, my name is Bettina Fisher. I live here in Washington D.C. I am director of strategic programs at School of Communications (SOC) at American University." Bettina handed the microphone to Renee. "Hello, my name is Renee Fisher Gibbs. I also live here in D.C. I am Senior Property Manager at Barnes, Pardoe, Morris & Foster. We are Betty's daughters."

Bettina told the audience the story of how she learned about my role in history. When her class studied Brown v. Board in high school, the teacher told how Warren County High School came to be integrated, and she told the class that Bettina's mother was the lead plaintiff. Bettina explained how shocked she was to learn that information. She asked the teacher if she was really talking about her mother, Betty Fisher? The teacher told her, "Go ask your mother."

Up to this point, my role in history was my secret. I explained only what my children needed to know. I didn't tell my children the whole story out of fear that they would have prejudices and carry on a legacy of hate. I worked very hard to teach them love for everyone.

Renee told how her almost-White complexion was a blessing and a curse at the same time. When she hung out with her Black friends, she was called names by White children. When she was with White people, they said things about African Americans that broke her heart. Renee explained that she grew up in a community of country people who didn't understand race. She said, "I felt like Rudolph the Red Nose Reindeer, and the kids at school wouldn't let me play in the reindeer games. When I moved to D.C. after college, I found friends who accepted me, and yes, they let me play in the reindeer games. I still cry every time I see the film because I know what my mom went through."

Renee and Bettina had broken the ice, and people in the audience began to tell their stories.

The 2017 Samuels Library presentation stands out for several reasons. First, because it was in Front Royal, Virginia. And it marked the tenth year of Phoebe and me presenting together.

I had learned that showing the documentary made presenting much less stressful for me. Five professors attended that event from several colleges and universities throughout the United States. My first-born grandson, Eric Jones, was also in the audience, along with Ariyanna, my first great-granddaughter. She came over to speak and sit with me. With a grandmother's heart and love, I couldn't send her back to her dad, so I took her by the hand and introduced her to the audience. I also introduced the little girl who played me in the film: Tanesia Renee Fisher Davis, my granddaughter.

During the question and answer period, someone asked, "How much progress have we made since February 1, 1960?" I didn't think about the specific date in the question, and I went on to answer the question as it related to my life.

When I finished answering, a woman came to the microphone and introduced herself as Marilyn Lott, one of the college students who sat at the lunch counter in Greensboro, North Carolina, on February 1, 1960, in an effort to integrate the lunch counters. She said she almost got kicked out of college. She whispered to me, "We are the unsung heroes."

We ended the presentation by singing "Amazing Grace." As we sang, everyone began to hold hands, and for a little while, we looked like the Beloved Community in Front Royal, Virginia.

After the presentation, the family gathered at a restaurant owned by Tommy, my grandson Eric's father. Phoebe's cousin Tim and my grandson Derrick got to know one another. Phoebe and Eric had an opportunity to get to know each other better. I pray that we created a lasting memory for Ariyanna. James and Janice were there as our faithful family and partners in creating the Beloved Community. The town that had brought about so many painful memories and heartache, 57 years later inspired a beautiful memory for the Kilby family at the table of brotherhood.

PHOEBE: It was meaningful to present at the Culpeper County Library in 2015, in the very county where my ancestors first enslaved people. Some African American Kilby relatives that neither Betty nor I knew came to the presentation. Now that we know more about how Malinda Kilby enslaved Sarah and Juliet, I would like to go back to Culpeper to add to the story and show them "Sarah's Brick." My cousin Tim could also present more about the Kilby family tree than Betty and I knew in 2015. I think that Rappahannock and Madison counties might also be ready for the truth about enslaving there.

I think that Betty's emphasis on creating Dr. King's "Beloved Community" is an appropriate ultimate goal for society's practice of restorative and transformative peace with justice.

BETTY: One last presentation experience—Phoebe and I were invited to address the Fauquier County NAACP in Warrenton, Virginia. An audience can make all the difference. I usually receive as much encouragement as I give from participants in the audience. The question and answer period is almost always a rich exchange of information among participants.

You never know who is in the audience. This time a European American psychiatrist was present. He said he had offered his services to parents and children who attended the newly integrated schools. However, no one took advantage of his services. He wanted to understand why no one took him up on his offer if it was such a traumatic experience.

I thought about how I could answer as honestly as possible. I said, "We believed and trusted God." A preacher on the front row began to clap his hands, and the audience followed with a loud applause. The psychiatrist sat down. But the minute the event was over, he was in front of me wanting to talk further. One on one, I could tell him that it was hard for our parents to trust White people with the minds of their children, even while they were getting an education. And, yes, our parents drew on their faith and trust in God to take care of us.

He found it hard to believe that we could go through the journey of integrating a school as children and come out normal and well adjusted. I informed him that I was not normal, nor was I well adjusted, and that I had spent most of my life healing from the trauma of integration. He left our conversation, bought the book, and brought it back to me to autograph.

Every one of our presentations was special, and each one brought us closer as the Kilby family. Phoebe and I stayed in each other's homes, only to find that we were more alike than different. I wondered if Phoebe could cook because we always ate out when I stayed at her house. When Phoebe came to spend a night at my house on our way to the National Conference on Dialogue and Deliberation in Austin Texas, we took her out to dinner. In the middle of dinner, I asked, "Phoebe, can you cook?"

We both laughed because we both had the same question in mind. We had each left our cooking days behind as we worked and traveled. But when I got custody of my grandchildren, I had to come out of retirement and use my domestic skills. Today I have retired my domestic skills again!

Q&A WITH BETTY AND PHOEBE 17

AUDIENCES HAVE A way of asking questions and offering comments that get right to the heart of things. It's a gift to us to see into the lives—and the concerns and observations—of the people we engage with while telling our stories. Here are a few

Betty and Phoebe speaking at a conference, November 2, 2019.

samples of give-and-take that we've had. We certainly do not have all the answers and continue to learn every day. We will always be learning.

QUESTIONS ASKED TO BETTY

Q. **What do you do to get yourself through the hard times, when some White person treats you bad?**

A. First, I remind myself of who I am. I am a child of God full of grace and beauty.

   Only God's love and mercy matters. There was a time when Black and White people hated me. So I developed my own criteria about people. I try to treat everyone with respect. But before I let people into my circle of friends, their spirits will determine whether they are friends or foes. Sometimes I am wrong in my judgment and I get hurt. You get hurt enough times, you become a pretty good judge of character.

Q. **What do you do when you are triggered by something and remember some of the hard times you have gone through?**

A. I find myself in a state of panic! I am that little girl again, and my reactions are the same as the little girl experiencing the trauma. Most of the time I realize that it's all over, and everything is all right.

Q. **Why don't you hate White people?**

A. My father wouldn't allow us to hate. He taught us that hating was like taking poison because someone hated us, and the only one to die would be us. I no longer have the capacity to hate anyone. There are actions that I dislike, and I sometimes react to them in a negative manner. I am still human and a work in progress.

Q. **What about those boys who raped you in high school?**

A. When I wrote my book, I went back to Warren County High School and sat on that very stage. Inside myself, I was putting those boys on notice. By writing the book for the public to read, I was saying, "I am here. I have survived. I am not afraid anymore. I forgive you."

Q. **Why do you even bother coming to the table? Why is coming to the table important?**

A. Coming to the Table has been a major venue for healing and self-analysis. Participants bring up issues from the depths of their souls in a warm supportive environment. We can talk these issues out of our souls and see that we don't have to be afraid because we have killed the dragon that haunted us. CTTT is important because we have a misunderstood and hurting nation of people.

Q. **Do you have hope for the future?**

A. Yes! My hope for the future is simple. It is my dream that one day we can live in the Beloved Community based on justice, equal opportunity for all citizens, and love for one's fellow human beings.

QUESTIONS ASKED TO PHOEBE

Q. **How did you figure out that your family were slave owners? How can I do this?**

A. I provide some answers to the first question in Chapters 5 and 9 of this book. Rereading these chapters might also help you answer the second question.

More specifically about your second question, the goal is to build your family tree by first finding the names and locations of residences of male ancestors who lived prior to 1865.

Why male ancestors? Because U.S. Census records that display slave ownership are most often found attached to the male heads of households. You can find information about the number, gender, and ages of persons enslaved by these male heads of household in Census years prior to 1865.

In most cases, you will not find names of enslaved persons, but I have seen a few cases in the Census where some names are recorded. There are instances, as with my great-grandfather's brother's widow, Malinda, where a female may be listed as head of household and have slave data shown.

I think the most important place to start building your tree is with your living family members. If you have grandparents or great-grandparents that you can talk to, begin collecting their stories now before it is too late. I had only one aunt left, my Aunt Lucia, and she provided a great deal of information, plus some physical evidence.

Many families have old Bibles in which they recorded births, marriages, and deaths. Some families often have a member who is particularly interested in history and genealogy and can provide you much of the information you need.

Next, go to the local library and access Ancestry. com. (This is not an endorsement of Ancestry.com. There are other organizations that you might use, including Archives.com, FamilySearch.org, MyHeritage.com, etc.) Most libraries have a subscription to Ancestry.com that you can access for free from their computers. Of course, you can purchase a subscription, which allows you the opportunity to do your research any time you want. As you get serious about your research, you will find this essential.

On Ancestry, you can search for your ancestors and where they lived, perhaps starting with a grandparent or great-grandparent, and then checking birth and marriage records to identify their parents. Someone may have entered your family tree on Ancestry and done much of the work already. I was lucky to find my European American family tree already posted online on a website set up by a distant cousin. I found that by just Googling my family name.

It is always helpful as well as fascinating to visit the historical society and local courthouse where your family lived to search birth, death, and marriage certificates, wills, and property records. Some local governments recorded slave sales among their property records, and there is a movement to put all these records online. The library of the state where the enslaving occurred will also be a font of information.

This is just a brief summary of ideas for genealogical research. Most libraries offer courses in genealogical research. It may be a good idea to take one of these taught by someone more knowledgeable and skilled than I am. I consider myself an amateur. I warn you that once you start this research, you might find yourself addicted to it!

Q. Any genealogical research advice for someone descended from enslaved persons?

A. As a European American, I had an easy time finding my ancestors because official record systems have historically been set up in ways that favor European Americans. African Americans will likely find that my research journey as documented in Chapters 5 and 9 is different from what theirs turns out to be. I can give you some hints, but it might be best for you to start with these two resources: OurBlackAncestry.com and Afro-American Heritage and Genealogical Society, at aahgs.org.

If you are a descendant of enslaved persons, genealogical research is more difficult, because most official records prior to 1865 do not include much about your ancestors in ways that are easy to find. You can easily find information in the U.S. Census back to 1870. That is when formerly enslaved persons first appear. The 1870 Census is key to providing early information on your family. In addition, birth, marriage, and death records for family members during the late 1800s can provide information on the names of the parents who were formerly enslaved. But to find more information about those enslaved persons, you will very probably need to know the names of their enslavers.

For many African Americans, interviewing older members of your family may be the most important resource. A good book to use to prepare to interview your older family members is *Grandmother's Gift of Memories* by Danita Rountree-Green.

Q. **Do you feel bad that your family members were enslavers? Do you feel shame for this?**

A. Yes, I do feel bad that members of my family were enslavers, and I feel some shame about this. I know that I am not to blame for their enslaving. As Betty has said, "You did not enslave anyone." Yet, my family participated in slavery and in Jim Crow oppressions. I am sorry that they did, and I feel compelled to make amends in some way. In addition, I am not blameless regarding my own racism. You can read about what I have done with these feelings in Chapter 18.

Q. **Why are you dwelling so much on the past, on slavery? That's over and done with. You need to address racism today.**

A. As William Shakespeare said, "What's past is prologue." We learn from studying history. And I believe that if we don't face our own and our family's history, we may very well repeat some version of it. That said, I do not believe that I dwell only on slavery. I spend most of my time thinking about and working to address racism today through Coming to the Table National and through my Asheville, North Carolina, local CTTT group. I write about this in Chapter 18.

Q. Do you ever question what you are doing?

A. I question what I am doing with Coming to the Table every day. I wonder whether I am doing any good in this work. I must take my cues from African Americans to determine whether what I am doing is helpful to them.

Q. You and Betty have spoken about how people can get caught in cycles, going back and forth between being a victim or an aggressor in conflicts. Can you say more about how to break free from these cycles?

A. Maybe a better way to talk about this is to use the language, "people who have been harmed," rather than "victims," and "people who have harmed others," instead of "aggressors." The label "victim" implies someone with no power. Few of us want to be called a "victim." Nor do we want to be labeled an "aggressor," though we may admit that at times we have harmed others. Using different words may open paths to thinking and feeling differently, and eventually changing behavior.

The STAR Snail Model below shows a path toward reconciliation. Betty and I have taken some of these steps, and we continue on the path. But note that this is not a step-by-step process that one must take in the order presented. If you try it, you will find that your path will likely vary somewhat from the model, as has Betty's and mine.

Also, Betty and I have not referred to the model constantly as our relationship developed. We were informed by the model when it was presented in that Coming to the Table class long ago. Then we let our relationship progress naturally.

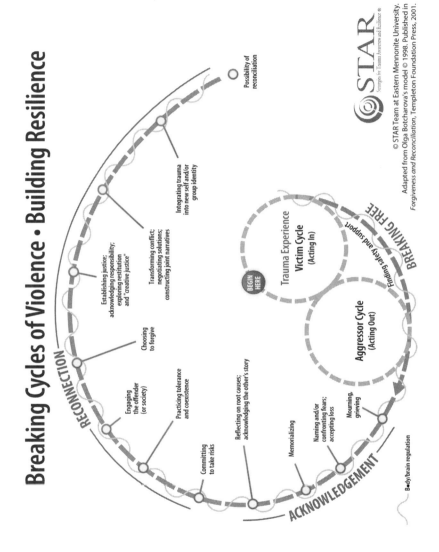

"Snail Model" – Breaking Cycles of Violence - Building Resilience, Strategies for Trauma Awareness and Resilience Program. Center for Justice and Peacebuilding, Eastern Mennonite University.

We have found it helpful to first be aware of the major action steps shown in large capital letters around the outside of the model.

BREAKING FREE

In order to begin a path toward "reconciliation," one must choose to break free from the cycles of harm. The first step of breaking free is to find enough "safety and support" to lift your foot off that high platform and step into the unknown.

ACKNOWLEDGMENT

Then the really hard work starts, where you and your partners in the journey begin to honestly acknowledge the harming that was done, who did it, and who was affected.

RECONNECTION

This honesty can lead to seeing the other person as a human being, and then reconnecting as human beings. Apology and forgiveness seem to me to be a necessary part of reconnection. The last steps of reconnection must address the injustices.

Positive changes that support justice can lead to the "possibility of reconciliation" for you, your partners in the journey, and your community. At least, that is how I understand and have experienced it.

More specific steps appear in the model in smaller type on the inside of the spiral. Betty and I made our choice to break free when I sent that email and she responded, "Hello Cousin." My CTTT connections and my peacebuilding training have provided the "safety and support" I needed to send that email. Betty's faith and training in nonviolence provided her what she needed to be open to me.

Early on, Betty, her brother James, and I jumped into "memorializing," when we worked together on commemorating the 50th Anniversary of their integrating Warren County High School. While this was a celebration of the success of their school integration efforts, there was also "mourning and grieving for losses," as Betty acknowledged her classmates who had passed away.

The commemoration led to revitalized activism to lobby the school board to name the school James and Betty integrated after their father. We had jumped to the end of the model with an attempt to "create justice." So you see you can take some steps out of order. This involved "taking risks" sooner than the model suggests.

But then when that justice action was not successful, we decided we had to step back and host the "Our Shared History" dialogue. That is where many of the ACKNOWLEDGMENT and RECONNECTION steps of the model occurred. We "acknowledged each other's stories" and "reflected on root causes." We "named some of our fears." We "engaged the offender" and "practiced tolerance and forgiveness." This led to more efforts to "create justice" by installing the historical marker in front of the school.

Betty, James, and I, and the rest of the family, have continued to wend our way along the many steps of the model's path. I think Betty and I would agree that the possibility of reconciliation is truly within our grasp.

QUESTIONS TO BOTH BETTY AND PHOEBE

Q. **Using terms like "White" and "Black" is racist. Why don't you always use "African American" and "European American?"**

A. **PHOEBE:** This is always a difficult topic to address, because I believe there is no easy answer. Betty and I have participated in many group discussions where what terms to use to describe ourselves has been discussed. Each group has come up with a different solution. What is acceptable depends on who is present. Not everyone of the same race thinks alike on this question.

A term that offends one person may be perfectly acceptable to another. And what is acceptable changes over time as people think and re-think issues of race.

I like using "African American" and "European American," but when speaking and writing, using these terms repeatedly can become cumbersome and awkward. I find myself lapsing into "Black" and "White," as do many other aspiring anti-racists I know.

When I speak about historical events, I find it more authentic, less hiding of the truth, to use the terms used at that time, terms like "Negro" and "Colored."

I don't have an easy answer for this question. If the term I use offends you, I beg your forgiveness. I can change the offensive term in real time, but not in a published book.

A. **BETTY:** I don't believe the terms "Black" and "White" are racist. I was brought up using "Colored," "Black," and

"White." I was "Colored" up until James Brown started singing, "I'm Black and I'm proud." After that, I said I was "Black." I was grown and educated when we started using "African American." The terms "African American" and "European American" fit only in more formal settings or writings. I am an American, my grandchildren are Americans, my great-grandchildren are Americans. We were born in America or on American military bases. Bottom line, we are Americans.

Q. **My parents brought me up not to see race. I see everyone as part of the human race. I don't understand why people are racists. So, what's my role in all this?**

A. **PHOEBE:** Yes, you may have been taught this, but I suggest that all of us who have lived in the United States have been exposed to a great deal of overt and covert racism and have soaked some of it in whether we realize it or not. This deserves self-examination. Do you never discriminate between people of different races? Are you sure you have no biases whatsoever? Try taking this test to see if you have any hidden biases: www.tolerance.org/ professional-development/test-yourself-for-hidden-bias

Beware if someone says that you have said or done something racist, and your reaction is to be defensive. Ask questions of the person and yourself. They may be able to help you identify biases that you did not recognize. This tends to be true of all of us, so try to view such conversations as a learning experience, not an attack.

Your role, first of all, is to self-examine. I recommend these two helpful books—

1. *Stamped from the Beginning*; and
2. *How to be an Antiracist*, both by Ibram X. Kendi.

A. **BETTY:** In 1945 when I was born, race was very much an issue. My birth certificate identifies me as "Colored." Educate yourself, learn history, take Phoebe's advice. Your role is to educate yourself about American history and to associate with people who come from diverse backgrounds so you can see the whole picture.

Q. **This country is never going to change. Just when African Americans seem to be getting ahead, the "White man" rises up and pushes us down again.**

A. **PHOEBE:** I see this pattern, too. But I am not willing to give up working for change.

A. **BETTY:** The title of my brother's book is *The Forever Fight*. I tend to believe that we will always be fighting in the workplace. This country is made up of individuals. There is always someone lurking in the workplace with the power to discriminate and disenfranchise another human being. However, for every racist, there are three good, decent human beings. Our job is to continue to fight for what is right.

Q. **How is this restorative justice? Your families never had a good relationship, so what are you trying to restore?**

A. **PHOEBE:** You are right. My family once enslaved Betty's. We are certainly not trying to restore that relationship. I refer you to Chapter 13, where I discuss the relationship of restorative justice to Coming to the Table.

A. **BETTY:** Justice! The Kilby Scholarship, which you will read about in Chapter 18, gives the descendants of my ancestor Juliet an opportunity for better jobs and the ability to fight injustices.

Q. **What advice do you have for a young person like me?**

A. **PHOEBE:** Betty and I are both over 60, so maybe this all seems irrelevant to you. But Coming to the Table has young members. Two of our board presidents have been in their 20s. I suggest you read Chapter 12 in the book, *Slavery's Descendants: Shared Legacies of Race and Reconciliation*, edited by Dionne Ford and Jill Strauss. Chapter 12 is written by Fabrice Guerrier, a Millennial, who eventually became the CTTT board president.

A. **BETTY:** Take Phoebe's advice! Nothing compares to you learning to know individuals from diverse backgrounds so you can navigate in a diverse world.

Q. **I am inspired by your story. How can I "come to the table"?**

A. **BETTY AND PHOEBE:**
Go to this website: www.comingtothetable.org. Sign up to be a member of Coming to the Table and join the CTTT Facebook page. CTTT has local groups meeting all over the U.S. The website offers the list of groups and contact information for their local leaders. If there is no local group in your area, use the contact page of the website to ask for someone to talk to. You can also attend one of our National Gatherings, which are announced on the CTTT website.

For good background to the movement, read *The Little Book of Racial Healing: Coming to the Table for Truth-Telling, Liberation, and Transformation* by Thomas Norman DeWolf and Jodie Geddes.

REPAIRING THE HARMS

18

BETTY AND PHOEBE

COMING TO THE Table (CTTT) defines reparations "as the taking of affirmative steps to repair the historic injustices done to African Americans during slavery, Jim Crow and later." We view this broadly and believe it includes any manner of steps taken by individuals, communities, and/or the nation to address the harms against and oppression of African Americans in the past right up to today.

Some might object to the word "reparations," saying that you cannot repair what is broken. Others fear that "reparations" can only mean taking money out of European Americans' pockets and giving it to African Americans.

Here is how the two of us are participating together in repairing the harms.

PHOEBE: When I consider reparations, I think first about Betty's and my families and how blended they are becoming. Yes,

I still talk about my White family members and my Black family members, because our society makes these distinctions, and because we grew up living apart, not even knowing of each other for so long. We had separate histories. But these histories, since we first met in 2007, are being woven together.

Early on, we started to participate together in each other's important family events. Betty and James invited me to the big family celebration of their mother's 95th birthday. The room was filled with over 100 family members, and I was one of them. When James became the pastor of a church, he invited me to his induction ceremony. It was an all-day affair with services, meals, and ceremonies at the First Baptist Church of Little Washington, just down the road from the county courthouse where I first discovered James's great-great-grandmother Juliet and great-grandfather Simon in the court records. My cousin Tim met James for the first time at this event.

Betty's mother, Catherine Ausberry Kilby, at her 95th birthday party.

I was touched when James came to my mother's funeral in 2014. I was able to introduce him to my mother's family and even a Bryn Mawr School classmate who came from Baltimore.

BETTY: I remember one year, long before I met or knew that Phoebe existed, a group of friends and I started an African American Historical Organization. We researched and wrote about the African American journey in Front Royal and Warren County, Virginia. We published our findings in a book titled *Freedom Road*.

At one of our Black History programs, I presented my findings on the free Negroes of Warren County. I had a picture of one of the ancestors in a dress befitting only the White ancestors; however, here she was. I wore a dress like the dress the Black woman wore in the picture.

I talked about how the first Africans who came to the English colonies were free. They came as indentured servants. When I read the last names and told the story of the free Negroes in Front Royal and Warren County and how they came into existence, there was a lot of excitement.

One time when we visited Rappahannock County, Phoebe and I sat on the front porch of Old Man Dick Finks' house. This was probably the first time I thought of Old Man Dick Finks and smiled. He wouldn't have recognized me, but he might have guessed that I was James Wilson Kilby's daughter. Or perhaps he would have recognized me as Mary Ella Smith Kilby's granddaughter. We survived his dominance and oppression. I bet he turned over in his grave as Phoebe and I sat on the porch of his house talking like two fine ladies.

PHOEBE: Since connecting with Betty and James, we have returned to Rappahannock, Culpeper, and Madison counties a number of times together. None of us ever lived there, but our parents did.

The first trip I took was with James and his mother, Mrs. Catherine Kilby. We talked about the places we knew and what our families had told us, or did not tell us, about what happened there. Mrs. Kilby had some distant memories about where Simon Kilby had lived. We traveled up and down F.T. (Francis Thornton) Valley Road, where Old Man Dick Finks's farm and the farm where my father grew up, are located. We went south into Madison County, because I had found a deed from 1898 showing Simon buying land there. We traveled round and round, but things looked different to Mrs. Kilby. She could not find the little road she remembered that led to Simon's home. Still, the trip was a step toward reparations as we shared stories as descendants of enslavers and enslaved who had once traveled these very roads.

The next time Betty and I visited the same area, we were with a Swedish Public Television crew. SPTV had contacted Coming to the Table because they wanted to film a segment about descendants of slavery connecting. They particularly wanted to film in front of an enslaver's house or land. At this time, I did not know where Malinda Kilby Thornhill's land was located, but my Aunt Lucia had taken me to visit my great-grandfather Jack Kilby's land. We drove along the narrow country road and parked in the driveway of the old house where Jack and Ellen had lived. I did not know who owned the house and land now.

Betty and the film crew pushed me to knock on the door to ask if we could do some filming. I had no idea what I was walking into. Would I be met with a shotgun and a demand that I get off his land? I knocked on the door repeatedly, but there was no answer. I must admit that I was relieved. But the film crew did not want to give up.

They positioned their camera on the very narrow road shoulder and started asking me and Betty questions. After a few minutes, a pickup truck rounded the curve and slowed as the driver, an older White man, rolled down his window. Uh-oh. I went up to the window. He said this was his house and asked what was going on. I started spouting Kilby names in the hope that this person would recognize them and think that perhaps I was okay. He knew all those Kilbys. It turned out that he was also a descendant of Jack Kilby. We were distant cousins. But before I knew it, Betty was on the move.

BETTY: This was the first time I saw Phoebe nervous about what we were doing. And it was probably one of the first times that I was really excited about what we were doing on our new adventure. I knew Phoebe worried that my feelings would be hurt, or that I'd be harmed by the White Kilbys.

I stuck my hand in the window and said, "Hello, Phoebe and I are cousins. Are you my cousin, too?"

He said, "Sure." His grandson, who was sitting in the truck on the passenger side, was as excited as I was. I did what Phoebe had done earlier—mentioning everyone named Kilby that I could think of, hoping this man would also know at least some of them and think I was okay, too.

I asked the young Kilby if he studied history in school? He said, "Yes." I told him we were rewriting the history we've been taught and telling the true and complete story. I told him that I was a descendant of the slaves that his ancestors once owned, and that Phoebe and I are coming to terms with this history by looking back and moving forward. He replied, "Cool." This was truly a wonderful experience, and I was seeing something that I never expected to see—White and Black Kilbys getting to know each other in a natural sort of way. It was a welcome change.

PHOEBE: The more I've gotten to know Betty and James and all their family, and the more I've learned about my and my family's complicity in their oppression and the oppression of other African Americans, the more I've felt that I should do something to make amends.

I would say to Betty, "I think I should do something to make up for what my family did to yours, for enslaving your ancestors." Betty would reply, "You didn't enslave anyone. You don't need to do anything more than you are already doing."

My response: "But that doesn't seem right. That lets my family and me off the hook. Don't you think someone needs to make amends for the harms? I think it should be me."

To which Betty would say: "No, you've done enough."

But I could not let it go. What might Betty accept as reparations? Then it hit me. Because she and her family valued education so much, wouldn't a scholarship fund that benefits the descendants of persons my family enslaved, wouldn't that be of interest? When I posed the idea, Betty had to stop and think.

BETTY: I worked very hard to achieve the education that was taken from me. I was selfish and satisfied that I had taken back my education. But I knew I had to recognize my Post Traumatic Slavery Syndrome and its impact on the future of my children. I had begun to wonder how I was going to finance my grandchildren Derrick's and Gabriel's education beyond high school. I began to panic. As a grandparent raising grandchildren, I was not prepared for their college educations.

They had experienced their own personal trauma, and they were not in a position to receive scholarships by traditional means.

So I said yes to Phoebe's scholarship idea because I was realizing that my PTSS was reaching beyond me to the next generation. Again, Phoebe was God-sent.

PHOEBE: So I set about to establish a scholarship fund. I thought it ideally should be an endowed fund so that it could benefit people long after I was gone. It seemed that access to funds for college would be most beneficial, and that the funds should be for a two-year or four-year school. I wanted to support port vocational training, as well as more traditional academic studies. The only criterion for eligibility would be that the recipient is descended from persons enslaved in Rappahannock, Culpeper, or Madison counties, Virginia. Preference would be given to those descended from persons enslaved by my Kilby ancestors.

Betty's granddaughter, Gabriel Byrd.

I checked with Betty and James all along the way to make sure that they thought the fund would be truly considered reparations.

Since recipients could attend any school of their choice, the fund did not have to be housed at any specific university or school.

Betty's grandson, Derrick Byrd.

I checked the NAACP website and found that they awarded scholarships. Their funds were held and administered by the POISE Foundation in Pittsburgh, Pennsylvania. I met with the POISE staff and decided that this was where the endowed scholarship fund should be housed. I liked that the entire staff was African American.

The Kilby Endowed Scholarship was established in 2013 and gave its first scholarship in 2014 to James's grandson. It has given scholarships every year since, to Betty's and James's grandchildren and to grandchildren of some of their cousins.

My cousin Tim and other members of my family are giving or have pledged to give to the fund. In 2018, with Tim's help, I developed genealogical standards for proof of descendancy from enslaved persons as specified by the fund. Some people were applying and just saying, "Yes, I am descended from these persons," but they provided no proof. While I did not like the idea of making applicants jump through genealogical hoops, it would not be fair to award scholarships to persons who did not show they were qualified.

I added family trees developed by Tim to my website https://acommongrace.org/ so that applicants simply need to provide birth certificates for themselves and their parents that show descendancy from one of the persons on the tree.

Betty and James agreed with this approach. I hope to make other changes in the future, including setting up an all-African American Kilby Scholarship advisory board to the POISE Foundation to review applications.

BETTY: This was the only award that both my grandchildren, Derrick and Gabriel, received at their high school graduations.

Most scholarships are awarded based on merit. Texas scholarships are awarded to the top 10% of the graduating class.

Derrick insisted on taking Advanced Placement (AP) classes. The regular classes did not challenge him. He had to be challenged to be successful. He played trombone in the school band. He enjoyed the demands of practice and performing in the band. But he gave up his trombone when he graduated from high school, stating that it was time to get serious about his future. Derrick chose to go to Hill College, the local community college. The scholarship and financial aid paid for his first two years there. He earned an Associate's degree in the Spring of 2020 and will continue his education at a four-year university.

Gabriel, on the other hand, wanted to go to a Historically Black College or University (HBCU). She did not fall into the top 10% of her class. The Kilby Scholarship, financial aid, and student loans are financing her education. She was accepted by three colleges and chose Texas Southern University.

Derrick and Gabriel were not the first or the only ones to receive Kilby scholarships. They have cousins who are also receiving them. Our ancestors are living on and continuing to impact this generation. Our ancestors have taken us from slavery to freedom. We appreciate our White Kilby family and what they are doing through these scholarships.

PHOEBE: One thing I like very much about the POISE Foundation is that they are not just scholarship administrators. They are truly interested in Betty's and my story. Karris Jackson and Shirrell Burton of POISE asked if they could visit with us in Virginia to see where the enslaving occurred. About that time, BBC News contacted Coming to the Table about doing a film segment on Betty and me. So the POISE staff, Betty, James, my cousin Tim, the BBC News crew, and I went on the journey together, ending up at a farm once owned by Malinda Kilby. You can view the film here: www.bbc.com/news/av/world-us-canada-48679403/ her-ancestors-enslaved-mine-now-we-re-friends

From the left, James M. Kilby, Betty Kilby Baldwin, Phoebe Kilby, Tim Kilby, staff from POISE Foundation. Standing on land owned by Malinda Kilby on which Betty's and James's ancestors Juliet and Simon might have worked.

Betty and I still have a lot to explore and do together!

For example, in November 2019, Betty and I presented our story at a conference of the Shenandoah Valley Battlefields Foundation (SVBF). The conference was entitled, "The Long Road to Freedom: African Americans in the Shenandoah Valley—The Centuries-Long Journey from Slavery through Civil War to Civil Rights." In late September of that year, a little over a month before the conference, I received an email from a member of the Shenandoah Valley local group of CTTT. He had once been a member of James Kilby's Historical Education Movement (HEM) with me. He included an article from the *Winchester Star* newspaper that reported on the erection of a new Confederate monument by the SVBF at the Third Winchester Battlefield.

Oh, no, what had Betty and I walked into? I called Betty immediately.

BETTY: My husband and I live in our RV. We travel all the time. Every October, I go to Virginia to celebrate my mother's birthday. She was about to turn 101 in 2019. The SVBF presentation had been on my calendar for at least six months. The two events would coincide well. Then I received the email Phoebe forwarded from the local CTTT group.

As I was growing up, I would sometimes ask Daddy if I could do something. Before giving me an answer, he would say, "Let me sleep on it." My initial response to the email and to Phoebe was, "Let me sleep on it." Now that I'm retired, I don't get in a hurry or real excited about anything. I rely on my heart more and more.

My brother James had originally put me in contact with SVBF. I had good vibes from the gentleman at SVBF as we planned the event.

My husband and I have memberships in various recreational parks where we park and sleep in our RV overnight as we travel. Even though things are supposed to be different today, I don't ever forget how dangerous it was in the past to travel throughout the South as African Americans. When we're traveling, I sometimes use my Passport America Resorts because I can usually find a park just off the main route. I call the resort to book the reservation, and then call again as we get close to it.

When we arrived at the Haas-Cienda Ranch RV Park in Poplarville, Mississippi, we were greeted by three flags, each as big as day—the Mississippi flag, the American flag, and the Confederate flag. We had already paid for the night. To get a refund, I would have to go into the office.

We were tired and ready to rest for the evening. My husband said, "You have never run from a fight, so I know you aren't going to run now." He took me by the hand, and we went to the office. I did a quick, silent evaluation and decided it was safe to stay there for the night. But all the while, I kept asking, God, what are you trying to tell me?

I called Phoebe back and told her that I wanted to proceed with the presentation, despite the Foundation having just put up a new Confederate monument, and my husband's and my recent brush with the Confederacy. If we canceled our presentation in protest at such a late date, it would reflect badly on us. Participants were coming in part because we were on the program. We are about change! It is up to us to take every opportunity to show all sides of history.

PHOEBE: Betty wanted me to speak up about what the Shenandoah Valley Battlefields Foundation had just done. At the beginning of her part of the presentation about her role in school desegregation, she talked about traveling in her RV from Texas to Virginia for the conference. "On the first day of our journey to Virginia, we started out at 7:30 a.m. and drove 360 miles in a little over five hours to Poplarville, Mississippi, where we were faced with those three huge flags, among them the flag of the Confederacy. In a split second, we decided to stay instead of run. I was on my way to tell you about a war that had no name. The war that no one wanted to talk about, in which the soldiers were children marching to get an education."

We decided that I would tie this part of Betty's presentation into comments at the end about our concern regarding the Foundation's recent erection of a Confederate monument. "Our family, our community, our American history is multilayered. We applaud SVBF's efforts to bring to light some of this multilayered history, which has heretofore remained in the shadows. But I would like to leave you with something else to consider.

"Remember Betty's story of being confronted by a Confederate flag when she and her husband arrived at the RV park. Think about how she must have felt. So how do you think she felt when I had to tell her that, a little over one month ago, the SVBF erected a new Confederate monument complete with a Stars & Bars inscription at Third Winchester Battlefield?

"I hope that the SVBF Board reflects on this conference and this recent action—the erection of the monument—and reconsiders its approach to monuments and the telling of the history of this valley.

"Perhaps the Board might consider the opinion of Robert E. Lee. He declined to participate in the erection of monuments at Gettysburg. Responding to the monument planners, he said: 'I think it wiser moreover not to keep open the sores of war, but to follow the examples of those nations who endeavored to obliterate the marks of civil strife and to commit to oblivion the feelings it engendered.'"

The SVBF staff seemed to notice. Later, during the final panel discussion, I offered some ideas about alternatives to monuments on battlefields. I suggested that instead, each year at each battlefield, the SVBF could plant sunflowers in great swaths, one for each soldier who fought, or maybe one for each soldier who died. This would give visitors a visual feeling of how many fought and died there.

Another suggestion was that they do field research to locate all the large trees that exist today that were alive during the battles. Visitors could be given maps to help them find these "sentinel trees" and contemplate what these wise old trees had seen the foolish humans do.

Finally, and most importantly, I suggested that the SVBF produce a video about life for the people of the Shenandoah Valley before, during, and after the Civil War, giving ample attention to the enslaved persons. Like the video, "Wit, Will & Walls," it should include reenactments and commentary by historians and should be enriched by the arts—poetry, music, visual arts, and dance.

The SVBF Executive Director was furiously writing down my ideas. Afterwards, my cynical self said to Betty that I wondered if that was just for show. Had I really made any impact? Betty told me that I could not know who I—who we—had impacted that day. Yet another person had reminded me that the effects of activism can range far beyond what seems readily apparent.

As for the future, my CTTT friends in the Shenandoah Valley are keeping us abreast of developments there regarding the Shenandoah Valley Battlefields Foundation, their monuments policy, and their efforts to tell the story of slavery in the Shenandoah Valley. They want to make sure that African Americans are part of the planning and implementation of those activities. There may be future opportunities for Betty and me to be involved.

Meanwhile, I serve as a co-facilitator of a Coming to the Table local group in Asheville, North Carolina. We are a very activist group and are focusing our activism in three areas:

1. Reducing police brutality and the school-to-prison pipeline in Asheville and in Buncombe County;
2. Addressing health disparities and working for health equity in our area; and
3. Supporting expanded Pre-K education for African Americans.

This sounds like a lot for a small group to work on, but we partner with other organizations and thereby hope to make a difference with these actions toward reparations.

I hope that eventually our group will get to that place of reconciliation, where "Truth and Mercy have met together; Justice and Peace have kissed." It has taken Betty and me more than a dozen years to get there, though as we know, staying there will always be a challenge as well as a delight.

Betty and Phoebe enjoying each other's company.

BETTY: Every time I think my work down here on earth is done, God shows me that there is still work for me to do. My work doesn't stop, but the focus changes from one project to another. Now, we are two families, two histories joined together as the Kilby family, to tell one story of our common grace!

238

READINGS AND SOURCES

Afro-American Historical and Genealogical Society. https://www.aahgs.org/

Alexander, Michelle. *The New Jim Crow: Mass Incarceration in the Age of Colorblindness.* New York: The New Press, 2010.

Appiah, Kwame Anthony. "The Case for Capitalizing the B in Black." *The Atlantic,* June 18, 2020.

Aylor, Lillian Freeman. *I'll Get it Done: A Life Journey in Rappahannock.* Fredericksburg, VA: Bair, Inc., 2019.

Ball, Edward. *Slaves in the Family.* New York: Farrar, Straus, and Giroux, 1998.

Battalora, Jacqueline. *Birth of a Nation: The Invention of White People and Its Relevance Today.* Houston: Strategic Book Publishing and Rights Agency, 2013.

Berry, Wendell. *The Hidden Wound.* San Francisco: North Point Press, 1989. First published 1970.

Campt, David W. *The White Ally Toolkit Workbook: Using Active Listening, Empathy, and Personal Storytelling to Promote Racial Equity.* Newton Center, MA: I AM Publications, 2018.

Coates, Ta-Nehisi. *Between the World and Me.* New York: Spiegel & Grau, 2015.

Coates, Ta-Nehisi. *The Water Dancer: A Novel.* New York: One World, 2019.

Cleaver, Eldridge. *Soul on Ice.* Illinois: Delta, 1968.

Coming to the Table, "Vision, Mission, Approach, Values." https://comingtothetable.org/about-us/

Coming to the Table, "Reparations Guide." https://comingtothetable.org/reparations-working-group/

Davis, Fania. *The Little Book of Race and Restorative Justice: Black Lives, Healing and US Social Transformation*. New York: Good Books, Skyhorse Publishing, 2019.

DeWolf, Thomas Norman and Jodie Geddes. *The Little Book of Racial Healing: Coming to the Table for Truth-Telling, Liberation, and Transformation*. New York: Good Books, Skyhorse Publishing, 2019.

DeGruy, Joy. *Post Traumatic Slave Syndrome: America's Legacy of Enduring Injury and Healing*. Milwaukie, OR: Uptone Press, 2005.

Fisher, Betty Kilby. *Wit, Will & Walls*. Euless, TX: Cultural Innovations, Inc., 2002.

Ford, Dionne, and Jill Strauss, editors. *Slavery's Descendants: Shared Legacies of Race & Reconciliation*. New Brunswick, NJ: Rutgers University Press, 2019.

Gates, Henry Louis, Jr. *Finding Oprah's Roots: Finding Your Own*. New York: Crown Publishers, 2007.

Gates, Henry Louis, Jr. *Stony the Road: Reconstruction, White Supremacy, and the Rise of Jim Crow*. New York: Penguin Press, 2019.

Green, Danita Rountree. *Grandmother's Gift of Memories*. New York: Broadway Books, 1997.

Griffin, John Howard, and Robert Bonazzi. *Black Like Me*. Berkeley: 2010.

Hermence, Belinda. *We Lived in a Little Cabin in the Yard: Personal Accounts of Slavery in Virginia*. Durham, NC: Blair, 1994.

Hooker, David Anderson, and Amy Potter Czajkowski. *Transforming Historical Harms*. Harrisonburg, VA: Eastern Mennonite University, 2012.

Joiner, Lottie L. "A Soldier's Story." 50th Anniversary of Brown v. Board of Education, The Verdict on Equal Education, A Special Report, *CRISIS Magazine*, NAACP, May/June 2004.

Jones-Rogers, Stephanie E. *They Were Her Property: White Women as Slave Owners in the American South.* New Haven, CT: Yale University Press, 2019.

Kendi, Ibram X. *How to Be an Antiracist.* New York: One World, 2019.

Kendi, Ibram X. *Stamped from the Beginning: The Definitive History of Racist Ideas in America.* New York: Bold Type Books, 2016.

King, Ruth. *Mindful of Race: Transforming Racism from the Inside Out.* Louisville, CO: Sounds True, Inc., 2018.

King Center, The. "The King Philosophy." https://thekingcenter.org/king-philosophy/

Kilby, James M. *The Forever Fight.* Pittsburgh: Dorrance Publishing, 1998.

Kilby, James Wilson and Patricia Kilby-Robb. *The Kilby Legacy: I Stretch My Hands to Thee.* Front Royal, VA: Kilby Publications, 1999.

Kilby, Phoebe. "A Common Grace." https://acommongrace.org/

Kot, Natalia. "Jordan Hall Namesake: The Controversy." *The Virginia Advocate,* Charlottesville: University of Virginia, March 2014.

Lanier, Shannon and Jane Feldman. *Jefferson's Children: The Story of One American Family.* New York: Random House Books for Young Readers, 2000.

Lederach, John Paul. *The Little Book of Conflict Transformation: Clear Articulation of the Guiding Principles by a Pioneer in the Field.* New York: Good Books, Skyhorse Publishing, 2003.

Lederach, John Paul. *The Journey Toward Reconciliation.* Harrisonburg, VA: Herald Press, 1999.

Long-Higgins, Hannah. "Her Ancestors Enslaved Mine. Now We're Friends." BBC News. https://www.bbc.com/news/av/world-us-canada-48679403/her-ancestors-enslaved-mine-now-we-re-friends

Menakem, Resmaa. *My Grandmother's Hands: Racialized Trauma and the Pathway to Mending Our Hearts and Bodies*. Las Vegas: Central Recovery Press, 2017.

Moore, Paulette. "Wit, Will & Walls." Film. Winchester, VA: Shenandoah University, 2007.

Morgan, Sharon. "Our Black Ancestry." http://ourblackancestry.com/

Riggs, David F. *7th Virginia Infantry*. Lynchburg, VA: H.E. Howard, Inc., 1982.

Sharp, Gene. *Waging Nonviolent Struggle: 20th Century Practice & 21st Century Potential*. Manchester, NH: Extending Horizons Books, 2005.

STAR, Center for Justice and Peacebuilding, Eastern Mennonite University. "Strategies for Trauma Awareness and Resilience." https://emu.edu/cjp/star/

Whitlock, Craig, Leslie Shapiro, and Armand Emamdjomeh. "The Afghanistan Papers: A Secret History of the War." *The Washington Post*, December 9, 2019.

Wiencek, Henry. The Hairstons: *An American Family in Black and White*. New York: St. Martin's Griffin, 2000.

X, Malcolm and Alex Haley. *The Autobiography of Malcolm X*. New York: Grove Press, 1966.

Yoder, Carolyn. *The Little Book of Trauma Healing: When Violence Strikes and Community Security Is Threatened*. (Revised & Updated) New York: Good Books, Skyhorse Publishing, 2020.

Zehr, Howard. *The Little Book of Restorative Justice*. (Revised & Updated) New York: Good Books, Skyhorse Publishing, 2015.

242

ACKNOWLEDGMENTS

We wish to acknowledge the many people who contributed to this book and to our story. They include Betty's family: her husband David Baldwin; father James Wilson Kilby; mother Catherine Ausberry Kilby; brothers and sister, James M., John, Gene, and Patricia; and all of Betty's children and grandchildren. Phoebe's family also supported this work: her husband Barry Carpenter, sister Margaret, aunt Lucia Kilby, and cousin Tim Kilby.

We were patiently encouraged by many members of Coming to the Table, too numerous to name them all. But we cannot omit giving special thanks to Will Hairston, Susan Hutchison, Tom DeWolf, Prinny Anderson, and Shay Banks Young.

Educating and providing invaluable guidance was the staff of Eastern Mennonite University's Center for Justice and Peacebuilding (CJP), including Amy Potter Czajkowski and David Anderson Hooker. Without the encouragement we received from Howard Zehr of CJP, we might never have embarked on writing this book.

Judy Tole at the Rappahannock Historical Society provided invaluable assistance with genealogical and historical research.

We also offer our thanks to the people who hosted and shared their stories and experiences at our "A Common Grace" presentations.

And finally, we honor Dr. Martin Luther King, Jr., who continues to inspire us as our journey continues.

ALSO FROM
WALNUT STREET BOOKS

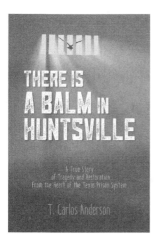

There is a Balm in Huntsville
A True Story of Tragedy and Restoration From the Heart of the Texas Prison System

by T. Carlos Anderson

A riveting nonfiction narrative, this is a true story of tragedy and restoration from the heart of the Texas prison system. Two 19-year-olds on a date are killed by another 19-year-old, driving drunk. What should happen? What takes place when victims of violent crime confront their offender, face-to-face? **$14.99**

5-Ingredient Natural Recipes

by *New York Times* bestselling author, Phyllis Good (creator of the *Fix-It and Forget-It* series)

Phyllis Good's cookbooks have sold more than 14 million copies, making her one of the bestselling cookbook authors in the U.S.

A hit on QVC and elsewhere! **$19.99**

For more information, go to: **www.walnutstreetbooks.com**
These books are available wherever books are sold.

ABOUT THE AUTHORS

DR. BETTY KILBY FISHER BALDWIN grew up in rural Culpeper and Warren counties, Virginia, one of five children. Thanks to her father's determination, she entered and graduated from Warren County High School after suing the school board, based on the landmark Supreme Court Brown vs. Board of Education decision of 1954.

Betty started her employment as a factory worker and climbed the corporate ladder to achieve executive management employment. After she retired, she wrote and published her autobiography, *Wit, Will & Walls*.

Betty has four children. She and her husband are based in Texas, but spend much of their time traveling the U.S. in their RV. Betty is actively involved in Coming to the Table, and speaks frequently with Phoebe about making connections across the racial divide to create a more just and peaceful world.

PHOEBE KILBY grew up in Baltimore, Maryland, where she lived with her physician father, mother, and sister. Phoebe had a long career as an urban and environmental planner, working on contracts with local, state, and federal governments.

With concerns about the morality and wisdom of war and a growing interest in peace, Phoebe studied extensively at the Center for Justice and Peacebuilding at Eastern Mennonite University.

A descendant of enslavers, Phoebe was inspired by the Coming to the Table movement to connect with descendants of persons her family enslaved. She is dedicated to helping others, European Americans and African Americans together, to uncover and explore the truths of their experiences and move toward racial reconciliation. With Betty, she continues to pursue a common grace.

If you would like to invite the authors to speak at an event or to a group, send an invitation to them at:
kilbycousins.com
